Fighting Just to Dream

Errol R. Reid

Copyright © 2021 Errol R. Reid

All rights reserved.

ISBN:

Book formatting by The Writery Ink, LLC

Bloomfield, CT USA

DEDICATION

Fear of failure is worse than failure itself!

Errol R. Reid

CONTENTS

Dedication	iii
Contents	v
Acknowledgments	vii
Daydreams	9
Dream Deferred	13
Durango	17
Alhambra	87
Yuma – La Paz	109
Florence West	170
Letter to You	201
About The Author	203

ACKNOWLEDGMENTS

I would like to thank everyone that was a part of this journey. The many individuals that offered their stories to be told. The many individuals that supported the completion of this book. Thank you to all the family and friends that offered support. Thank you to all readers and those who found a message in this book. May you find peace as you continue on your journey.

Thank you to my son, Mason who has been a driving force and inspiration to become a better man. Thank you to Lindsey who has been there during this entire journey. Thank you to Alma who has been my real guide during one of life's most complicated times.

Thank you to God. He is always Good.

Errol R. Reid

DAYDREAMS

Thick, dark clouds danced ominously across the evening sky. The sun played a tantalizing game of hide and seek. It was the middle of monsoon season, yet not a drop of rain had visited the soil. A few months had passed – nine to be exact. I asked myself, why do you love her so much? Was it her look? Her slender, athletic body with those sexy dimples perched just over her immaculate backside? Was it her youthful qualities? Those would eventually fade. Her God-- given blessings would be taken and that beautifully sculpted face would droop, her flowing black hair would turn to ashy-gray. I must have seen the true little girl inside of her. The very man who had sworn to protect her would be the one to hurt her. Her dad insisted on disciplining her to the extreme, yet he had no discipline himself. She felt scared of him, rather than protected. She resented him yet was more similar to him than to anyone else. She was stubborn; set in her ways.

Whatever it had been lost out to the captivating power of the ripples in the sand from last night's wind, as my attention diverted. I had heard those winds howling like a pack of wolves, all through the night. My mind bounced like a ping-pong ball as my thoughts darted, yet again. I wished I could just find a switch to turn that love off and put it to rest. Then, maybe I could get some rest too.

I had become so transparent to Wayne. He had come to know me as a brother and he knew I was hurting inside. I glanced down into the coarse sand. Neither of us spoke a word. He gazed off into the distance, adjusting his vision through the small rectangles that made up the fence. He too, was caught in a daydream that transported him far from our stark reality – prison.

The chatter of inmates could be heard in the distance; bustling about selling brownies, placing bets on football, and taunting one another over the card table. The smell of prison liquor, hooch as it was called, overwhelmed us each time Yardy popped the cap off the undercover soda bottle.

I scowled as I thought that such a drink couldn't possibly be healthy if the stench alone was so vulgar. It did its job though. The inmates were all laughing and telling jokes; red cheeks, watery eyes and all. They were all enjoying themselves while duck and goose were frozen in heartbreak. I closed my eyes and slipped off into a trance.

I heard the washing of dominoes two hundred meters away, along with the loud and obnoxious voice of West. He always slammed every domino he played. I imagined him shirtless, as he could always be found, for some reason. His gray, speckled beard explained the old soul that he bore. His spirit also appeared happy, as he always kept those around him deep in laughter, as if he were hosting a Def Comedy Jam. Returning from my trance, I managed to pull together a soft smile and turned to see what Wayne was up to. Maybe it was just time to break the silence altogether. The indiscriminate noise was getting too loud and I was scared of listening to my own thoughts any longer. I knew they might continue to tell me the truth, but I wasn't ready; it just wasn't the time. I already knew I had messed up over the years. I mean, just look at where I was. I needed no one to explain that to me – not even me!

My eyes scanned the room and landed on Wayne as he leaned against the antiquated phone box. His eyes were closed as if he was in a dream, but I knew all too well that he was only dreaming to lose his reality. As was the case with everything else around here, you had to fight even just to escape from your own mind for a minute and some Chicano was exemplifying just that. He had the nerve to ask Wayne for the phone that provided him comfort in that moment.

When I realized what he was doing, I gave him mine to keep the peace. Just then, Wayne forced his eyes open just enough to observe the slim-built Mexican standing squarely in front of him and exclaimed:

"Man, get out of my face!"

The unrelenting thoughts running through my head had long since chased my smile away.

Maybe I was a bigot to love? How did I get here? Take a good look at yourself and your forefathers. Your father is a womanizer. He lives with his wife but is separated and sleeps in an entirely separate room. Your grandfather is sophisticated, yet he's still a drunk. He too, lives with his wife yet sleeps without her. Was this what my life had in store for me?

This thought jolted me out of my dream-state. Why couldn't I fantasize like everyone else in here? They walk up and down these halls and fill them with smiles and laughter, as if they were at home with no worries. Why was I so serious all the time? Herb got it right when he told me I was a chronic over thinker. Was I even a dreamer, I wondered? It's possible I was not, but my forefathers sure were. If nothing else, it was a dream that bought my father's one-way ticket to federal prison for twenty years. My mother though, she was different as she preferred reality.

"Work hard. Burn the midnight oil," she would always tell me.

Whether she was running her small shop selling sweets, harvesting crops, or raising animals, my mother led by example. It was through her determination alone that she was able to send me to Munro College, Jamaica's most prestigious secondary school.

My mom never thought I'd turn out just like her – blunt, harsh and fiercely independent. I stopped accepting money from her at fifteen years old; instead, I bullied other kids at school, just as they'd done to me. I sold Gummy Bears to my classmates and I performed services for payment. Instead of waiting in long lunch lines, I would offer to put my connections to good use to retrieve and deliver lunches faster. Kids would pay me a fee for services such as this and this was how I made my money. I invested my money and bought a goat and a few pigs. My entrepreneurial spirit even led me to perform delivery duties where I brought weed to Kingston on school days. I made these deliveries to a relative's boyfriend and never spoke a word of it. I touched my second gun ever that same year. Hard worker. Burning the midnight oil. The principle was good, but I had no dreams and no goals; only fantasies. The sentimentalist in me was taught early on that dreams were impractical and led to nothing but disappointment; just like that time my grandmother promised me Nike Air Max's for Christmas but then sent me something different. Who wants to experience the high of a grandiose fantasy, only to be disillusioned shortly after? That would never be me!

The reality is that I still struggle today. Who am I? One thing's for certain – my identity continues to evolve on a daily basis and didn't stop or slow once it crossed the line of felon. Thislabel won't define me. Who shall I be? Where will my path lead? What will I become- a hard worker or a dreamer? Perhaps, I will even be both.

Today, I am transferring to a new state prison and in true "manly" fashion, neither Wayne nor I spoke a word of it. We shared a bond. We had an unspoken love for one another, but we just couldn't bring ourselves to say it. Maybe it was due to an ingrained fear of the prison culture we were immersed in. It was possible we had become soft. Whatever it was that day, we looked eachother in the eye, speaking silently, all the while gazing through time.

Fighting Just to Dream

DREAM DEFERRED

The massive house stood two stories tall on ten sprawling acres of lake view property. Its driveway paved with stones, neatly trimmed grass flanking its sides and cutstone walls with a wrought iron gate limiting access to the residence. An abundance of flowerbeds adorned the manicured lawn, most being in full bloom. Upon first glance, the super-sized hand-carved doors gave the impression that the owner was overly protective of his family. All the while, it was difficult to ignore the sheer beauty that the woodwork displayed. The door was that of three standard doors combined. They stood tall and impenetrable, with ornate gold handles. Contrary to the doors' intimidating façade, the curtains had not been drawn, allowing those standing at the entrance of the driveway a clear view into the house through the wide glass windows.

Midway down the horseshoe-shaped driveway and off to the side, two jet skis and a speedboat could be seen bobbing in the water. At an offshoot of the pathway, a three-car garage stood flanked by a pebble-dressed path that led to the water. The first door opened and a black Mercedes cautiously entered. The water-sporting equipment lining the wall allowed just enough room to pull in completely. The driver side door opened, but the figure did not exit immediately. Gucci dress shoes finally appeared, well-polished and with matching black socks. In a smooth motion, the driver finally alighted from the vehicle; a tall man with broad shoulders that filled out his expertly tailored suit brilliantly appeared. He was of brown complexion, immaculately groomed, with strong and storied hands. He pulled his briefcase out from the passenger side door and entered the living room. The side door was already slightly ajar, as if to anticipate his arrival.

He stood in the middle of the living room, scanning the lush gardens beyond the windows until his eyes landed upon a familiar figure in the backyard. Laura was beautiful inside and out. The sight of her took his breath away without fail every time his eyes fell upon her. Of average height, she had ebony skin that stretched tautly over her beautifully toned body. And her long dark hair was neatly fashioned into a chic bun that perfectly displayed her prominent cheekbones. Her athletic legs were crossed elegantly as she sat on a lawn chair sipping a glass of her favorite white wine. She turned her head and caught a glimpse of her husband admiring her from afar; the curve of her lips turning upward into the smile he loved to see more than anything in the world. He smiled tenderly back at his adoring wife as she threw him a cheeky wink.

He could hear the kids making noise off somewhere in the house. Even amidst the clattering of toys and the shrieking voices, he felt perfectly content – a far cry from the heightened emotions he had been battling all day. His shoulders settled gently as he breathed deeply, yet purposefully. His senses spun him around as he instinctively followed that familiar smell of his favorite steak and peppers sizzling on the grill. He could no longer stand his excitement as he slid the glass door back, stepping out onto the stone patio. To anyone else, it might just be a regular day. To him, it was anything but. He gently helped Laura to her feet with one hand. As he stared into her sparkling eyes, he physically felt his remaining stress evaporate into thin air.

He couldn't resist her; his hand wrapped around her waist and ended at his favorite spot, right above her buttocks where two dimples were perched. He bent his head toward her and kissed her passionately. When a modicum of Laura's composure returned, she simply said, "I love you too, babe," understanding that his kiss was a declaration of love in its own right.

His son barreled toward him, leaping into his arms with a fierce bear hug. At nine years old, his legs hung like a child five years his senior. His daughter, now four, was an angelic little figure who resembled her mom. They sat down to dinner together and he feasted like a man who had spent his life starving in the desert. After dinner, he bathed the kids and took great pleasure tucking them into bed. They said their prayers and he kissed each one tenderly on their foreheads. He walked back to his room and found Laura already tucked in on her side of the plush, pristine bed.

"Hurry up and shower, babe. I'm waiting for you," she said, smiling seductively.

The fragrant aroma of his freshly cleaned body filled the room as he returned in all his naked glory. He slid under the crisp white sheets and gently kissed her. Every touch was followed by a gentle moan. He elevated her body using one arm and she gracefully collapsed on his chest, her bosom pressing against his. Their bodies complimented each other's so well. Moaning and groaning softly, she kissed his neck and whispered into his ears. He slid down and caressed her full breasts, biting down on one while caressing the other in his big muscular hand. They made love with passionate abandon until they were deliciously sated.

Laura trailed her fingers over his chest ever so lightly, gazing up at her husband with unmitigated passion in her eyes. Smiling, he stroked her hair affectionately and kissed her forehead. The air was still but pleasant. The television had been playing but neither was interested. A show about the prison system played in the background, distracting him but only momentarily.

It had been five years now since he walked through those prison gates and vowed never to return. For too many nights, it was only possible to hold Laura in his dreams. But tonight, that dream was a reality and he would take full advantage of the moment together. He brought his attention back to her head purposefully rising and falling with the motion of his chest as he breathed.

No matter how deep he tried to bury parts of his story, he knew that his past was a part of him and forever would be. Prison played a role in that story; yet personal growth played a larger role in ensuring it would never make an appearance in his future, but his past reality lingered. His story goes like this....

Fighting Just to Dream

DURANGO

Phoenix, Arizona; Maricopa County Jail; D7 Pod.

A mesmerizing sea of black and white stripes accompanied by pink socks scurried about, creating an optical illusion that my mind was too tired to process. Inmates shuffled along obediently, ankles shackled and hands tightly clasped behind their heads. Their fingers intertwined as they marched on owning their destines. Each desperately gripped their processing paperwork – the only possessions allowed to them. Two detention officers walked casually behind the inmates as if they were taking in the scenery for enjoyment. I sat up on my bunk to better see what was going on outside of my barred window. The Lower Buckeye Jail next door was the first thing that came into view. My new reality of confinement had me desperately and unendingly searching for a way to escape. I was searching for hope.

The blinking red light atop LBJ sparked an ember in my mind and suddenly I was home with my girlfriend, laying together on the couch, watching television. She was enjoying a glass of wine while we watched 'Modern Family,' her favorite show. All was pleasantly serene until the officer jarred me back to reality shouting, "Chow time! Line up at the door!" My daydream had me dining on steak, but my reality had served me prison slop. Slop was a mixture of whatever happened to be on hand in the kitchen that day. Some mixtures included ground tofu, beans and breadcrumbs, while others were composed of "mechanically separated poultry and a dairy blend." Whatever it was, I had no doubt that a starving dog would reject it. For the most part, the inmates here had no such reluctance. I, on the other hand, refused to eat such a so-called meal and today was no different. My bunkmate accurately sensed my disinterest and stated in an eager voice:

"Reid, if you don'twant it, I'll take it."

"I got you," I replied.

This place was nothing short of a foundry, lumping inmates into two categories; better or worse. The jail system of racial segregation made things very difficult, especially because I had never experienced anything quite like it before. Blacks were called Kinfolks, Whites called Woods, and American-born Mexicans were Chicanos. Native Mexicans were known as Pisas and Native American Indians were Chiefs. Each racial group was comprised of a leader who governed his own people and was aptly called "The Boss." Each pod consisted of a group of racially distinct bosses that were expected to oversee their own people. Although it was a powerful position in its own right, serving as the head of a racial group was risky because it came with the possibility of a 2.5-year sentence if caught.

Usually, the officers had no problems with it until there was a racial riot where inmates or officers were killed or severely harmed.

I had done alright for myself thus far. After all, I wasn't the typical inmate. I was well-educated and held degrees. I was the youngest of three siblings born into a single parent household. My father had served twenty years in federal prison, so thirty days was more than doable.

I had been fighting just to dream from birth. I had arrived in America with only Fifty US dollars and had made thousands after only a few years. I had endured the lowest of lows and celebrated the highest of highs. What was the difference being here? I would survive, no matter what! I had made the best of my resources then and nothing was different now. I viewed my new environment as a challenge that would teach me more about others and myself.

In a well-run pod, inmates weren't oblivious to who the real head was, even when a decoy would be appointed to act as such. This ensured some level of security to the heads, but only from officers. An added layer of protection couldn't hurt. The heads kept a tight leash around their people to prevent race riots and all other sorts of mayhem from occurring. Race riots in particular were the worst fear of inmates and staff alike.

The grim reality was that the loss of life would occur during a riot. Some pods had a higher population of Kinfolks and vice versa. In such cases, the larger population would hold the controlling interest. They ran everything and if anyone dared challenge the laws then they were disciplined or had to roll up. Rolling up meant you had to ask to be transferred to a different pod. It was close to asking for protection so many inmates chose to be disciplined by their own race. Rolling up also carried with it the label that you are a troublemaker. Immediately entering a different pod, you were severely questioned and your paperwork shown. Showing your paperwork made you transparent as to why you were incarcerated. If not shown, you would be disciplined and asked to roll up to a different pod. Officers would get tired of the antics and place that inmate in protective custody.

Riots were vicious attacks that took place in a matter of seconds. They wouldn't usually last long but it was customary to find that someone was either severely hurt or was killed. There are even some occurrences where officers had fallen victim to a razor blade. It was never predictable for a riot to happen because on most occasions, it was started from a little argument over a card game or someone owing money. It was only predictable if someone had checked an inmate's paperwork and found he was a snitch or child molester. In that case, the code of a convict was not supposed to allow that inmate to live. It was a dog-eat-dog world and only the fittest of the fittest survived. Those that were weak were preyed upon and had to pay money for their protection or serve another for security.

Durango was composed of ten buildings, including an old warehouse. As the name suggested, the warehouse was a large dilapidated building that was transformed into inmate housing. Buildings One to Nine were so large they each housed four separate pods of inmates. The security office was nicknamed "The Bubble" for no reason other than it had tinted windows all around. The bubble faced all four pods and had television screens that showed live feed of what was taking place inside each pod. It was a popular location for officers to hang out and have a good time as most were lazy and would sit inside "The Bubble" all day. Every pod sat in the shape of an "L," with cameras mounted on the ceiling of each corner. The middle of each pod consisted of four tables. Once it was chow time, it felt like each of those tables had an invisible reservation. Everyone was distinctly separated by race. Cells were cramped with two bunk beds each housing four inmates of different races inside. The beds stood less than an arms-length away from one another. The door to enter and exit the pod was on the right-hand side and was controlled by the officer inside "The Bubble," just as most other aspects of our life were.

The bathroom was situated on the left of the pod. It was a central part of our daily life for many reasons. Upon entering the bathroom, two hand washers stood directly in front planted firmly against the wall. Aluminum sinks glistened even at night from the constant cleaning. Every race took turns cleaning it daily. The first washer was used purely to collect water for drinking and the other for maintaining hygiene. To the right sat a toilet that was only used for urination. Two showers seven feet tall stood immediately nearby and were flanked by two additional toilets. These toilets were divided by a single partition allowing for a minute degree of privacy while tending to business. Inside the bathroom from the urinal to the toilets was the only place the cameras did not capture. Naturally, that was where all the fights happened. As one would imagine, the first to leave the bathroom after a fight was usually the winner. The victor would prance around as a peacock basking in his victory.

Stripes, pink boxers, pink socks, and maroon sandals. All inmates blended together in a sea of visual similarity as officers worked tirelessly to strip us not only of our dignity, but our identity besides. Once a week, you were given a change of clothing. Even the heads of the unit had to partake in the bold pink fashion statement, which clearly signified much more than a mere fashion statement. It was a point that we were emasculated. We weren't men but boys being told when to sleep, eat, wake up, work out and when we would leave.

Our commands came from our authoritarian figure: the guard. They would march around calling us anything they wished, but if an inmate looked at an officer in a mean way, we would be on lockdown all day. No phones or TV. Other times, guards would even go to the extreme and take your commissary or not deliver it.

On one side of the pod, an old 12-inch bubble TV was bolted to the wall. Almost directly underneath the TV hung three phones, followed by two video calling booths. Video calling was introduced last year. It made it convenient to see your family, but the price per call was outrageous. I knew every inch of my environment thoroughly from being buried into my mind's eye. I was trapped inside four walls that I walked daily. The imagery was indelible as I worked out doing push-ups, burpees and scampered around the pod recording every corner calculating my strategies in case of a violent situation. Each cell was given a number, except Cell 56 which was skipped over.

Durango was originally run as a mental institution and it was said that a girl had committed suicide inside of Cell 56. Inmates compared chilling stories of the things they heard near the location of where Cell 56 was. The most consistently heard happenings had been those of sounds of a little girl singing and laughing, and the bouncing of a ball.

Although the different racial groups that made up Durango usually kept a strict divide, everyone mingled for a bit after meals in the evenings and on weekends. Chicanos were comfortable hanging out with Woods and would unite in case of a riot. Pisas were the same with Kinfolks. Everyone had their small group with whom they spent most of their time. My two friends were Shawn and YG. Both were younger than I was, but for some strange reason, we had gravitated toward each other since day one. YG, or Marvin as his papers said, was as small as a twig, but his heart was bigger than his little frame. He was a gang banger and this was his first time in prison. He had never been in trouble with the law before. He was a basketball player, a point guard in high school, and had dreams of attending Arizona State University prior to his arrest. He wore an Afro on top and a fade on the sides. He was black and Puerto Rican with skin that was of dark complexion. Even though he was skinny, he ate way more than I would and still couldn't gain a pound. I told him it was his stress level that was depriving him of gaining weight and he would laugh. To him, he was a gangster and gangsters didn't get stressed. That was the craziest street philosophy I had heard.

Shawn was even smaller in stature than YG. He was light-skinned; the pretty-boy type. He had been arrested years before and signed a plea for three years' probation.

Instead of a drug charge this time, he was here for a DUI. He and YG would always argue because YG was a Jack Boy (robber). On the streets they would have been enemies, but in here, they were the best of friends. YG was a year younger and definitely more playful than Shawn was. Shawn had become a father to a six-month-old baby boy that he had not yet seen due to his current incarceration. Being absent from his son became a driving force for him to turn his life around to become the man that he wanted to be. YG, on the other hand, was just stuck at the stage where he was down for anything. He just wanted to get out and get back to knocking on doors and ransacking houses.

Shawn and I were both from the East Coast. More important, we had signed a plea agreement for two and a half years in the Arizona State Penitentiary. YG had been going to court for his burglary charge and was given a bond. He was only here waiting to be bonded out. Shawn and I faced a more serious time and had a lot riding on our sentencing day.

Shawn was set to face the judge in two days. He wanted to read a short speech in front of the judge and he worked on it tirelessly.

"What's up, Rude Boy?" YG asked walking into my cell.

"Nothing, my brother. What's up with you?" I replied, rolling onto my back.

YG always came to wake me up in the morning. He thought it was funny until I would get mad. Most mornings, I would be up laying on my side staring at the wall. It was a deafening silence that made my thoughts so loud. It was also therapeutic and I could see and hear the flaws in myself. It wasn't the first time, but it was the first time I actually listened.

"Get your ass up. You're so big but you sleep like a bigass baby," he nudged my bunk laughing. "Go bother Shawn, Bro. He up yet?"

I picked up my hygiene supplies from the foot of my bed, then stepped into my slippers and headed to the bathroom. Shawn's cell was the last one on our block before entering the bathroom. I stopped just to say what's up real quick and then proceeded to the bathroom. He was still in bed, wrapped up like a mummy. He peeked through the end of the sheet and smiled a cheeky smile, his eyes half opened.

Returning from the bathroom, I saw YG was in Shawn's cell harassing him.

"Leave my little brother alone," I shouted jokingly. I jolted on his arm, nudging him into motion.

"Reid, every morning he does the same thing. Watch. Tomorrow he's going to come and I'm going to be gone. What's he going to do then?" Shawn ended.

"Shit, that only means Reid is going to have to deal with my bullshit," YG replied.

He and Shawn both laughed. I wasn't amused. At times, sleeping was my only getaway and at times not even that worked. It's one thing to live a nightmare, but to be asleep fighting through a nightmare could wake you up on the wrong side of the bed. Waking up from a bad dream could ruin your entire day. Our morning conversations were always spent talking about memories of when we lived in a free world. We would lose ourselves in laughter, reminiscing about the good times, until we were slapped back into our own realities by the call for morning chow.

Breakfast consisted of two loafs, soy peanut butter, a single jelly packet, a small box of milk, and an orange. This completed what inmates called a Lamo Bag. This was our first of two meals we were fed daily. It wasn't much, but it kept you alive. I found out if you starved yourself for three or four days, it would start to taste good. On a regular basis, I'd trade everything except my orange and milk with YG. A lot of inmates didn't drink their milk for various reasons and they would bring their milk to me. I would give them any extra item I had left over from my Lamo Bag. Milk and orange got me through most mornings.

Today was no different from yesterday. Fights were going down in the bathroom. Inmates were getting rolled up and sent to the hole because they were caught fighting. Inmates that owed money or commissary items were going to protective custody so they wouldn't get the shit beat out of them. In such situations, they would be 'smashed' beaten for two minutes by two individuals their size. The Heads gave the permission. In prison language, we call this a 'green light.' Somehow, all these rules didn't make any sense to me. Everyone here had done something wrong or had been accused of it, yet they wanted to set rules themselves. The rule system only made sense to the Heads as they collected 'tax' commissary from card games and commissary stores run by inmates. They were literally just as the IRS. It was a capitalist society outside these walls and inside wasn't much different.

Being an out of state inmate, I was more neutral. In the case of a riot though, I would have my brother's back. I was definitely more outgoing and laid back than other people native to the state. The politics didn't interest me. Somehow, I still caught the attention of others, prompting all of the heads to invite me into their office. I entered suspiciously and reluctant.

Every head, except the Kinfolk, was present in the cell. I was a little tense, as you never really know what can happen in this place.

"Reid, calm down. You're good," the head of the Pisa said with a smile. "Have a seat. *Relájate*," he continued.

"I'm good," I replied standing sideways in the cell doorway.

"We have been watching you and we like how you carry yourself and everyone respects you. We have voted to make you Head of the Kinfolks. We all selected you because you're a better candidate than the current Head. It's yours if you want it."

The Chicano head ended with a blank face yet eyes that seemed so dark. Staring at his teardrop tattoos under his eyes, I politely declined.

"No, thank you! I'm leaving here soon anyways, plus I'm from out of state. I'm not down with all the politics. I'm just running with it for the time being because that's the rules," I explained.

I turned my head slightly to find YG in the thick of the crowd. I noticed that all of the Kinfolks displayed faces of curiosity. YG's face said more as his facial expression communicated 'I'm ready when you say go, bro.' I smiled at him and shook my head, to tell him that there was no need for all of that. The heads all spoke amongst themselves and concluded that their offer remained on the table for me to consider and whenever I was ready, I just had to let them know. I wanted nothing to do with such a role. I was on a more positive path and being in jail, I saw nothing but negative involved in politics and racial segregation. The few commissary items you were paid were far less than the headache you dealt with daily. Knuckleheads could make your life a living hell, but if your people respected you, they would fall into pocket and respect themselves and others, limiting the chance of any altercations between races.

I walked back to my cell. My cellmate had been on the edge of his bed. He was peeking through the door just enough to see what had been going on.

"You alright, Reid?"

"Yeah!" I abruptly replied, ending the conversation before it began.

YG walked in clapping, his hands still turned up. When wasn't he?

"You good?" he asked, cocking his head in an aggressive manner as he asked the question.

"Celly, can I talk to YG in private real quick, please?" I asked him, picking up his slippers and placing them in front of him to assist in his exit.

"Yeah, I'm good," I explained as Shawn walked in and asked the exact same question YG had asked. "They wanted me to be the head but I said no. That's all."

"Oh, I thought dudes was on some bullshit," YG said. "Just

know, brothers had your back, Rude Boy. You a good dude whether you an out-of-towner or not," he ended giving me a dap. "Real shit!" Shawn added followed by another high intensity handshake. They both sat on my cellmate's bed and we changed the topic to a more serious situation. What was Shawn going to say to the judge, come tomorrow?

Morning came and YG was surprised to find me already up. I hadn't slept much at all last night. I was up talking with Shawn about his speech and points to touch on. We kept questioning the facts of what his reality just might be. Two and a half years for a DUI was awfully extreme. He wrote his speech that he planned to present to the judge in hopes of a mitigated sentence. We rehearsed his speech for effect, hoping to drive home the point. He was taking responsibility for his actions but seeking a chance at freedom to be a contributing member of society and a father to his son. We talked until late in the morning. I doubt he slept because he woke me up when he was leaving for court at 3:30am. I shook his hand and wished him good luck. I prayed for my brother, my family and friends, and thanked God for the experiences he had given me thus far.

YG's facial expression confirmed the worried feeling I embodied. We were both nervous for Shawn. In two weeks, I'd be getting up at 3:30 am to go to court and face the judge who would decide my fate. A part of me questioned how dumb I must have been to put my entire life in another man's hands. I felt a part of the link was missing. Ever since my first day, we had always been together, the three of us. Today was very different. Shawn was going in front of the judge and faced serious consequences for his mistake. His future on the line, he would be on his own trying to turn his bad situation right. Maybe I stood to learn from his clever ways of getting a mitigated sentence? Was that even possible? My lawyer had pulled every rabbit out the hat thus far.

The day was a complete drag. I prayed he would have received positive results in court. Intensive probation worst case scenario. It was doable and at least he would be a free man to make his own choices. His son would also get to meet his father which was priceless. If that was his verdict, he would be in a position to execute all the plans he had immediately. Sadly, that was not to be the case.

Shawn entered the pod and my cellmate walked out to give us some privacy. Shawn sat on his bed and took out his sentencing paperwork. The judge had given him the maximum sentence of two and a half years.

"Rude Boy, this shit is crazy. The judge and prosecutor both looked at me as if my life story meant nothing to them. They didn't have a care in the world for what I had to say. It was like they had already decided that I was done. I felt I was sentenced before I even saw the judge! They didn't even give me a chance."

He shook his head, staring into the concrete floor. He made no eye contact and continued to speak.

"Two and a half years for a DUI," he repeated over and over in a saddened tone of voice.

YG was now standing next to him and leaning on the top bunk of the bed. He was looking at Shawn but he didn't utter a word. I didn't know what to say. I hadn't been at that point in life before: heading to prison. I fell silent in that moment. No words could suffice. Somehow, I pulled it together and uttered a phrase that my girlfriend had always said to me when things got rough, 'This too shall pass.'

"This too shall pass, my brother," I repeated.

The words had lost their power and the room became silent. I fell into a blank stare looking at the ground. I never wanted to feel like this ever again. Beaten and tortured by life. I began to remind myself to be strong, no matter what. Even when others would quit on me, I was never to quit on myself. Even if the judge gave me the maximum sentence, I was to pick myself up and recreate a plan.

Shawn's life was about to take a turn for the worst and as the room stood silent, he started thinking of what prison might be like. He let out a heavy sigh, followed by a long silence. "Brother, everything is going to be ok," YG said, breaking the silence. "You going to be alright. Two and a half will fly by and you'll be a free man before you know it. Teaching your son to be a better man, unlike my punk-ass dad," he laughed.

YG couldn't even be serious for a full conversation no matter the circumstances. He had to crack a joke or make fun of someone. Shawn finally mustered up a smile and his dimples popped alive in his cheeks.

"This Boy," he exclaimed, looking up at YG shaking his head back and forth. "Fuck it, Rude Boy, let me go take a nap and shake this feeling."

He paused as he stood up and stretched. He dapped us and walked to his cell. He understood he was embarking on a whole new journey filled with unfamiliarity.

Shawn was a good brother. I knew he would be okay in prison but nobody wants to go to prison, especially with a six month old son back at home that was now forced to live his life without his father by his side. I understood his biggest concern was being away, but my judgement was biased. At least I had the blessing of witnessing my son enter into this world, in addition to being able to celebrate both his first and second birthdays with him. I had those memories and many more and he was without any, just a few pictures. In two weeks, I stood the same fate and the judge would decide the outcome.

I woke up after a nap and check in on Shawn. I stopped by his cell door and turned around to see YG holding onto the barred windows. He was staring outside, almost as if he was admiring the view he had at home of his neighborhood. His body was present but his lonely eyes longed to be far away, somewhere peaceful and enjoying life. Shawn was up sitting on top his bed. He held a notepad and a pencil fashioned out of added paper for support in his hand. Every word that he wrote on that notepad was an instruction, a delicately composed melody of wishes for the future. He wrote every word so fluidly, as his thoughts were transported to paper before they had even processed in his mind.

"What's up, brother," I interrupted his attention from his notepad. "You good?" I concluded turning my attention back to YG's gaze.

"Yeah, Bro, I'm just writing my baby's mom. I'm letting her know what's going, even though I know my mom has told her already. It's essential that she know where my mind is. That way, we won't have any misunderstanding or arguments, especially when it come to my son."

He paused and scribbled a few words.

I had been there before. Torn away from the clutches of my son, but only I wasn't a victim. I had chosen to be separated from his mom. Now I would do anything just as Shawn would to be with his son.

"I really need her to hold it down," he explained.

I thought we were such hypocrites. We wanted our women to hold it down. To be heroines like our own mothers were. We knew what that suffering felt like being a single parent, yet we caused the same dilemma for our kids.

"I feel you, my brother. Get some work done and I'll swing by in a few," I said with a heavy conscience as I walked away.

His entire demeanor explained that his letter was of grave importance. I did not want to inhibit his progress.

"Wake up!" I yelled at YG. He jumped back startled from his peaceful daydream. I had finally managed to have some revenge

Fighting Just to Dream

in the form of a prank. He laughed then explained, "You're lucky it's you. I was ready to pop off."

He balled his fingers into a fist and backed up into a boxer's stance, fists up and bouncing from side to side. His older cousin had taught him how to box when he was younger. He too was locked up in jail and last YG heard was that he was fighting commissary fights for food. He had been the one to introduce YG to the life of crime. He was a burglar and YG looked up so much to him that he walked in his every step. YG countered my observations of himself as not one who was always ready to fight but fighting for the right reasons. He was fighting for himself, his own dream. He felt his father hadn't fought for him at all but left him and his mom abandoned after exhausting all their resources. Last he heard about his father was that he was in California now preaching at a church, married and he had a new family. Living with his father was hell. He used drugs and stole everything in the house. The worst part was he would beat YG's mom if she confronted him. YG had a real hatred for him that fueled his anger to the point that he would unleash on anyone for the least reason.

We decided to sit down at a table right in front of New York's cell, our backs turned towards him. Our view through the barred windows was of a single officer, walking up into our sight. He stopped and pondered something himself, looking down and resting his head in his hand. He continued walking after a few seconds but then disappeared from our view.

"Brother, I know you're always preaching this positive shit to me but it's easier said than done," YG stated, breaking the silence. He believed in two things; "eat, don't get eaten" and "find a way or make one yourself." These were his beliefs from the streets. I would also tell him that a CEO sitting around his big decorated mahogany desk held these same principles, yet he was not in the streets but making more money at a lesser risk of casualty. He couldn't see the picture I painted for him when we had these conversations. As cliché as it sounds, a person just doesn't know what they don't know. I would tell him that he would understand one day.

"See the bigger picture," I calmly stated, forcing him to think for himself.

"That's the shit I'm talking about. You and the parables. Man, I wanted to go to ASU but now with a felony under my belt, a community college is my only option. As a matter of fact, fuck that," he stopped suddenly.

His body spoke more loudly than his words as he pretended to put a clip into an imaginary gun and cock it.

"Get the fuck down. Give me everything if you want to live," his lips twitched as he barked at the barred window.

"What if you kick in the wrong door?" I asked him. "He already has his gun out and waiting for you," I continued.

"Bro, I've had my pistol since I was ten years old. I'm quick," he elaborated. His eyes grew darker and his pupils widened.

Two things that I saw happening down the road YG was traveling included losing everything to the authorities or to death. The nights spent up in the club popping bottles, wearing expensive clothes were not worth a day that I spent in jail. Especially not now that I had prison looming over my head as well. I love my brother, but I could also tell that his mind was already made up.

"Look at Shawn, Bro. In there writing to his son's mother. His son is six months old and he still hasn't seen him much-less held him. My brother is suffocating from incarceration and you still want to try the same routes. Success leaves clues just as failure does and if you don't get the clue from drug dealing it's that you'll be dead or in prison. This is the only place that you are sure to see. It's time we make better decisions rather than to continue become modern day slaves," I continued to plead with YG.

"Everybody isn't like you, brother. You got bread so you can say anything. You have your college degree and you're intelligent," he countered.

In rebuttal, I exclaimed, "I come from a single-parent home because my dad did twenty years! I chose this game, trying to finish what he didn't. I believed I was living the life, but all that shit was nothing because I'm fed slop just like everybody else! Everybody has a story. Mine isn't all glory and the truth is I am broke just like everyone else here. Get your mind right, brother. See, you still living based on image. A man that fails to plan, plans to fail. That up in the air shit isn't going to do anything for you nor me," I ended, tapping him on his shoulder.

Our attention was directed to London and Thatcher, both Woods, that took the spotlight as they both yelled out from the spades table.

"Set! I'm the king of this shit," London yelled.

He picked up his "Champion" spades belt that he had made himself. It consisted of cardboard, checkers pieces that lined the sides, and an ace of spades in the middle. Always the comedian, he held it up high in the air. To him, he had won a WWE wrestling match. London was usually quiet and kept to himself unless he was on boose bars. Boose bars were prescribed medication for the mentally disabled and psych inmates as a depressant. It was made to be a depressant but if inmates withstood the urge to sleep, they would be high for hours.

I was familiar with marijuana and understood parts of cocaine. Living in a jail in Arizona widened my drug knowledge more than I had ever imagined possible. Inmates used black tar heroin and China White, the street name for pure uncut heroin. Meth use was rampant and most inmates were walking zombies, for one reason or another. Many were literally skin resting on bones. I saw so much ingenuity simply for the purpose of ingesting drugs. Syringes made from a toothpaste bottle and cap with a lollipop stick as a needle.

Some inmates would ingest drugs into their anus called 'butt rockets.' I imagined that if the same efforts were put into more positive ventures, then the resulting effects could be limitless.

As I sat on my bunk, the concrete floor allowed my mind to wander to a carpeted living room. I was sitting on a plush oversized couch. The pine trees showed themselves as the blinds rattled from the central air, allowing a temporary view of the leaves swaying in the breeze. My girlfriend's favorite perfume captured my senses as she laid her head on my chest. We were in the middle of making dinner and watching 'Modern Family.' Two wine glasses sat empty next to my leg. I gently stroked her hair; from the middle of her head all the way back to the tip of her neck, occasionally tangling it. I rubbed her neck and blew softly over it. Her body quivered as she turned her cheek towards me and blushed. She stared into my eyes, yearning for a real kiss. It was more fun for me to play hard to get, which was just what I did as I watched her eyes twinkle.

Lying on the couch with my girlfriend was a peaceful memory of my favorite thing to do on Friday nights. Tonight wouldn't be one of those nights at all. Instead, I was covered in stripes, pink boxers, and pink socks to match. No comfy sweats or basketball shorts. No steak and bell peppers served atop a bed of rice. Instead, it was precooked rice that somehow still was undercooked, served with a side of slop.

"Reid! Jamaica!" My cellmate's voice had grown into a yell.

He smiled innocently and shook his head.

"Hey, brother. Did you forget we were having a conversation?" he asked.

I hadn't heard a word he had said for the past minutes.

"What's up, Curtis," I replied, apologizing for my absence. "I was gone, huh?" I asked.

"Not here at all. By the looks of it, you were somewhere better than this piece of shit. As a matter of fact, anywhere is better than here," he proclaimed. "But um, Reid, I know you don't eat your slop. I'll trade you rice for it," he ended.

"Alright, I got you, OG," I replied.

"Thanks, brother," he ended satisfied in the deal he just closed. He smiled and fixed his towel under his neck and laid back down on his pillow.

I had two other cellmates. John and Pablo. Like I said, everybody in here has a story.

John was tall and skinny. He told everyone that he was a contractor and owned his own construction company. He was the boss and he built houses and renovated them. He professed himself to be a millionaire but he was here for meth. He owned a big house in the country and had horses and a stable. He had no teeth, but that didn't stop him from eating. As skinny as he was, he never turned down any extra food. He was also a Wood.

Pablo was rarely ever in our cell. He was always with the other Pisas. He barely spoke English and was very humble. He would always hand me his milk in the morning, saying, "Leche for you, my friend."

"Muchos gracias," I would reply.

He would crack up because of my Jamaican-Spanish accent. He was here for possession of a firearm. Being that he was illegal, he stood the chance of deportation if convicted. He explained that he carried a pistol after being robbed so many times in his own neighborhood. He was a landscaper and owned his little company. He made a lot of money working hard but was targeted because the Chicanos in his community knew he was illegal and feared contacting the police. He carried a pistol to protect himself, his family, and his property. He never had any previous record here in the United States or Mexico.

Pablo was no taller than 5'6" but weighed about 180 pounds. He had a wife who worked a minimum wage job because she did not have papers herself. He was the father of five daughters who were all born here in America. If Pablo was related to Pablo Escobar, I would not be surprised in the slightest. They looked so much alike. Pablo was very well-mannered and was always very thankful and appreciative if I ever shared anything with him.

Curtis was a Wood. He wore a Fu Manchu beard. His hair receded into the middle of his head, yielding a large bald spot. He was 56 years old and had been widowed the year prior. He was always cracking jokes but was habitually grumpy after every nap. He would curse his probation officer and the state for offering him two and a half years for under a gram of meth that the cops found in his pants pocket after he had complied to being searched. He had borrowed the pants after he helped a friend move into his new apartment and needed a change of clothes. He was pissed that he had consented to the search and was now locked behind bars. He spoke of his sisters constantly. The one that he spoke of most was bed-ridden and dying from cancer. All he spoke of was wanting to be home before her big surgery that might save her life. He wanted to squeeze her hand and show his support.

Curtis and his other sister had a falling out years back and she had stopped speaking to him. Her last words to him were, "How does it feel to lose another sister and I'm not even dead yet?" to quote his exact words. He got teary-eyed every time he spoke of her. Whatever caused their tight bond to break had him very remorseful to the point he would cry. He felt he wanted to die from the deep pain he endured daily. He would medicate using boose bars or anything else that he could get his hands on, but it wasn't enough. Reality would set right back in. His momentary relief felt worse when he returned to reality.

He had been homeless for over three years. He lived in the

desert inside of a huge tree in downtown Phoenix and also by the canal's edge. He would always say, though, that he had been to Hell and back while living next to the El Mirage River. He had been stung by scorpions, shared makeshift beds with snakes, encountered dead bodies, ran from the police, and came face to face with coyotes. Since his arrest, he found out that he had cancer. His problems were becoming more than he could bear, but he still cared more about his sisters than himself. He wanted to die so they would live.

The doctors at Durango had attempted to remove his cancer cells but didn't get it all. He would see medical daily for change of bandages and his regular dosage of drugs. Today, the doctor did an x-ray and found his tumors were growing back. This was a big source of his stress and he slept more than anything lately wrapping his towel under his chin and covering his face. He repeatedly said that he didn't care about dying because he died when his wife died. He had even been shot from close range and although he survived, he still failed to see his life as a blessing.

Curtis had used every drug known to man. He had tried to overdose more times than he could count, but he failed every time. This led Curtis to believe that he was simply immune to drugs; he couldn't do the job correctly or that God had a plan for him. The loneliness that he spoke of since the passing of his wife was simply unbearable to Curtis. He owned nothing but a bicycle and a few items that he had stored at one of his kids' apartment. He had hidden a backpack under some bridge in El Mirage that contained some important survival items that were useful when homeless.

"A tenth of meth, my pipe and lighter, of course," he would grin as he told his stories of being homeless . "There is no feeling like good dope, Rude Boy," he would end. Now relaxed, he closed his eyes then rolled over on his side, facing the wall. I knew every time he turned to the wall he would cry. I felt sad for him.

The cell fell silent for a few minutes before the officer shouted over the monitor, "Lock down for chow! Lock down for chow!" Inmates ended their card games and dispersed to their cells. Evening chow always brought tension with it. Inmates had not eaten since the first chow of the day and they wanted to be fed. Any inmates who lingered for lock down would be yelled at. A simple misunderstanding could land someone a good ass whooping in seconds. A very good day could turn into a riot at the drop of a dime. Today was no different.

Liberia had already been in a bad mood from his phone conversation that he had earlier. His attitude was straight "no bullshit." The fact that the phones were taken away immediately after his bad conversation since a Wood had disrespected a female officer did not help the situation at all.

"Lock down!" an inmate yelled, imitating the officer's demeanor.

"Shut the fuck up," Liberia responded, standing in his cell doorway. He stared from his cell, grilling the cell the yelling came from. "You must be a fucking cop. Y'all always run to your cells quickly for food. Fuck food! None of y'all told your race to check themselves before the phones got taken away," he exclaimed.

I stood up in my cell doorway. Liberia, dark as coal with broad shoulders, clenched his left hand into a fist. His neck veins stood at attention as he breathed heavily. Liberia had not been here three days yet and this was already the second time he had been ready to push any issue if anyone was ready to take it there.

The weekends were always like this. Loud bickering and fights, especially when we were placed on lock down for someone's stupidity. Liberia had a point, but the way he was exercising his point made him a target. The tension that built up was thick as smoke. The weekend emotions had everyone walking around either overflowing with anger, or avoiding the ones that were. Liberia turned around and mumbled as the locks to the door buzzed over and over. Saved by the bell; The officer came walking in doing his rounds before chow was served.

Liberia grabbed his shirt and struggled to put it on as if he was fighting it. Everyone lined up by their cell number to receive food. His words were directed towards Thatcher.

Thatcher loved fooling around but he stood silent as everyone collected their trays. Thatcher was a Wood that played around even in a homosexual way. He had no filter to what he let out his mouth. His jokes were mostly racial and sexual. At the present moment; however, he was at a loss for words. Even the officer could sense the tension as Liberia stared Thatcher down. I took my tray and went back to my cell. YG had the job of trading slop for rice. We traded our slop for rice in accordance with our new tradition of making burritos on Tuesdays and Fridays. I gave my slop to my cellmate.

"Hey, Reid, if there are any leftovers available after you take care of your people, hook me up, please," he requested, rubbing his sick arm with a sad face. He lifted his arm and shot me an invisible dap as he left. YG and Shawn walked in with their trays full of rice.

Shawn was leaving for prison on Monday, so today we were going to eat a hefty meal. Our plan was to make oversized burritos, drink sodas, and bake a cake. I had paid London, Head of the Woods, to make me a big cake for Shawn's departure. Everyone stared inside our cell and made comments as they walked past. They noticed we were making burritos and put their orders in for leftovers. This was pretty much the routine every time we cooked something.

Shawn was in a better mood. He shook the funk. I thought to myself that if he could get his head wrapped around going to prison and not be warped by all his emotions, then maybe he would be alright. Maybe we were just going through the motions pretending it wasn't reality. Nevertheless, we made burritos using hot pickles, beef sausages, chili beans, hot pretzels that we smashed on the floor to crush into pieces, mayonnaise packets, salt, pepper, and jalapeño cheese. We shook the ingredients together in a garbage bag that the morning porter had stolen for this specific purpose. The cake was made from cookies, brownies, soy, peanut butter, and the wheat bread that we traded at chow. The main ingredient for cake other than cookies was a soda. The citric acid was what made the cookies expand or rise then topped with jelly packets and snicker bars. A slice of cake could run you from a $1.20 to $2. Many people survived financially from making cakes and brownies to fill those who had a sweet tooth.

We all celebrated Shawn's departure by having a couple bottles of soda and laughter. For the few hours I forgot where I was. We ate burrito after burrito, until we could not even fit another bite. YG was finally defeated as he held his stomach to display how full he was to the other inmates. To eat like we did cost a lot of money that most inmates couldn't afford. The whole pod started laughing as YG began his full decent outside the cell lifting his shirt to show off his gluttony. His stomach was twice the size of a man his size. We laughed so hard as he joyfully played around and entertained.

All the meals we ate together, I had never seen him full before. Satisfied we had eaten one of our best meals, our souls were full of joy. We had forgotten that we were in jail. We shared our leftovers with everyone that asked to have some. We laughed and joked together in the dayroom, spreading our unrecognizable happiness on a weekend. My cellmate came running over as if he hadn't just had stitches removed from his arms. I had already put his burrito on his bed, but in jail, first come first served.

"Thank you, brother. To be completely honest with you, all this shit scares the hellout of me but I have no other option but to own up to my responsibility. Going to prison might not even be that bad," Shawn exclaimed.

He was finding his way through the dark unknown. We shook hands as YG came running to our table excited. Liberia and Thatcher had fought. He brought Liberia some of the burrito and cake and was informed of the intricacies to the matter. Liberia had whipped Thatcher's ass and Thatcher had the battle wounds under his eyes to prove it.

My intuition had told me that while I was laughing and joking, something else was going on. There was a group of inmates sitting in front of the tv, but their attention was toward the bathroom. That never meant anything good. Liberia was frantic as he walked into the cell and called us to come inside.

"You think Thatcher's sick?" he asked.

"Sick?" I asked, confused by the question.

"Yea, sick like Hepatitis C, HIV or something," he explained.

"I don't know," I replied, "but if he were, you should wash your hands immediately and thoroughly. Use some chemicals even if you have to. The few teeth he has left are all bad. You never know what's going on with somebody," I ended.

Everyone burst out laughing at my teeth comment. Liberia held his hand up to his face to check his knuckles for cuts and abrasions. He had a concerned look on his face. He picked up the shampoo bottle at the end of the bed and went to the bathroom to wash his hands. He dropped off the bottle of shampoo, returning just seconds later. I guess he wasn't too concerned after washing his hands because he was eating cake YG had given him out of his hand.

Today had definitely lived up to the hype that is associated with the weekend. The weekends were always ominous and dark. The weekends invited trouble that inevitably came. I was just happy to have had a little party for Shawn to enjoy even in the midst of chaos. Before lockdown, I had to hurry to use the phone so I could top off a successful weekend of no drama with a great conversation with my girlfriend. It was always nice hearing her voice before bed. I read my bible and prayed for my family and friends, before trying my best to fall asleep.

Sunday dragged on into Monday. The tension relaxed as inmates were getting released or had the chance to by paying their bond. Others were already at court pleading their cases, signing pleas, or delving into their trials. For others, like Shawn, today meant a trip to the 'Pinto' Prison. His first stop would be Alhambra, where he would go for classification. Alhambra was a Level Two and Four Yard. All inmates held for classification were locked down for 23 hours every day. They would only get out twice a day for 30 minutes, once to have lunch and then to eat dinner. Breakfast was served to you as you laid on the floor next to a toilet. Possibly once every two days you were allowed to walk around the yard. At Alhambra, there would be no phones to communicate with the outside world. Writing letters was your only option. If you hoped to have any communication back, that wouldn't occur as you'd have left to a different yard by the time it was delivered.

Shawn was in a good mood this morning. We didn't know whether he would leave today or tomorrow as at times the buses would be full. I expected the not-knowing to cause him anxiety but it didn't bother him at all. Maybe to him what was the difference? He was already locked up. The day he would get out would be the only day that mattered anyways. When we talked last night, he was looking at his time positively or at least trying to anyway.

"At least no more slop," he had said over and over.

He felt the need to accept his reality rather than running from it. Life had happened and he was prepared to make lemonade out of the lemons he was given. A part of him began to accept responsibility for his actions rather than looking back trying to change things. 'What ifs' had disappeared and it was more 'what I'm going to do is.' He was set on writing as many songs as possible. The world would know him and he had a perfect story of the "comeback" to tell.

YG woke me up as usual and together we went to check on Shawn. He was mentally and emotionally drained. Prison could make anyone bi-polar and go from being schizophrenic to being normal. He lingered and took his time before finally getting up and going to the bathroom. YG and I had requested our last game of spades before running the chance that Shawn might leave. Shawn was my partner and we quickly jumped ahead winning the first game nine to four. No help by me, of course. I was a poor spades player and everyone knew it. They still loved playing me because I was so competitive that I wouldn't give up. I wanted to win. I had to win. I believed there was always a chance to comeback no matter how much I was down.

I had been learning how to play this game throughout my time here. I wasn't into card games. I hadn't played games at all before prison. I played sports but being locked up all day long drew me to get involved. It allowed time to go by a lot faster being occupied. We continued to play. YG dealt the cards and we began placing our bid. Instantly, the monitor sounded. The officer began calling out cell numbers and immediately after she yelled, "Roll up!" The whole pod listened silently. I could not ignore the overwhelming feeling of anxiety that swept over my body as we waited in silence.

"55, bed 4, roll up," the officer announced.

"Brothers, this game is to be continued," Shawn smiled.

I could see right through that smile, as I knew he was just doing what he had to do to keep it together. It was customary for friends to help the person leaving with his bedding. YG and I grabbed his bedding and sheets and brought it to the door. We shook hands and said our goodbyes as everyone scrambled for new beds they wanted to move into. Others were just trying to say a few words to their friends or family members being housed in separate pods. Some were being released and some were headed to prison. Wherever the journey was taking them, this destination had expired.

Kites were slipped under doors to pass information. YG hid Shawn's extra blanket under his mat in his cell. He ran back out in time as the door opened and Shawn stepped out. He dropped the bedding in the bin outside, right next to The Bubble. The officer came out from The Bubble and checked to make sure all of his bedding had been brought out. I shook Shawn's hand one last time and gave him a big brother hug. YG did the same. YG's eyes watered. He couldn't hold back the tears although he would undoubtedly deny so later on.

Shawn walked outside carrying his manila envelope full of legal paperwork and letters he had received.

"Likkle more, Rude Boy," he tried to mimic my Jamaican accent. "Let me know how court goes for you. Hopefully, I will be getting a letter from you telling me that you're home!" he exclaimed.

The officer shouted at him to keep it moving and close the door.

"If worse comes to worst, then hopefully we end up in the same pinto," he ended.

We both laughed.

"Stay safe, brother. I'll let you know what's up for sure," I shouted as the door slammed shut.

YG and I watched through the glass window as they cuffed his ankles and wrists. He held up both hands, still holding his manila envelopes under his armpits to wave goodbye. The officer lined the inmates in a queue and went over their names and inmate numbers to confirm each inmate's identity. They were seated on the ground until a transporting officer arrived. Later, they took the whole crew along to the holding tank. Shawn was beginning a new journey. This was one he had to travel on his own. His life was a notepad and only he had the pen to write his story.

I spun around from the empty dayroom where the inmates were all just being held. I caught Curtis' eyes looking in my direction. He stared at me and mumbling soft words to those at the table with him.

"Reid! They took your friend, huh?"

He had asked a question and made a statement at the same time. A part of me felt like I had lost a brother and Curtis could see it written all over my face.

"Yeah," I replied, walking into my cell.

Pablo was on his bunk, snoring away. I sat on my bunk and stared into the happiness I had created while looking through the barred window. I laid down hoping that I wouldn't share his fate.

"Reid, let's go finish the game," YG said as he tapped my bed. "Don't do that. Pablo's sleeping, bro," I stated firmly, grabbing his arm.

I shook him a little, then released his arm when I realized what I was doing.

"Your cellmate out here saying you must be mad they took Shawn. Shit, I'm still here. You better let them know that and don't grab me like that again," he insisted jokingly threatening with his fist.

"You are one crazy brother for sure," I muttered, thankful for him. He was always there to make me forget my environment. "Let's go, little homie!" he teased.

He needed to play cards and forget his reality as much as I did.

I spent the majority of the day playing cards and watching TV. I read and wrote for quite a while to pass the time. Writing was therapy for me. It not only helped me to escape the physical bars that barred my body, but I felt I was talking to a therapist every time a single ink hit paper.

With no one in sight from the pod being on locked down, I peered into the blinking light for inspiration. It brought my focus back to the single most important book in my life and continued reading the bible. I read Proverbs. I read it over and over. The wisest man in the world, Solomon, had written the book of Proverbs. I wanted all the wisdom it had and sought it by dedicating my evenings to meditating on his words. I read the bible to attain a level of knowledge and wisdom, in hopes of better understanding life and my surroundings. It talked about friends, relationships, and of dealing with people in authority. Many inmates read the bible and would also attend prayer meetings. Similar to my own experiences, other inmates noticed their spirits too were lifted as they became closer to their religion, but it was always temporary. It was hypocritical behavior. We would leave prayer meetings and go right to the gambling table or disrespect someone or sometimes masturbate right after in the shower.

"What's your last name?" the Marshall asked in a stern voice.

I hesitated as he held my license in his hand. My picture was clearly displayed and my identity stated. Maybe he wanted to confirm my identity, even though my name was not difficult to pronounce or understand when read.

"Reid. That's what it says on my ID," I hesitantly replied.

I was still handcuffed with my hand behind my back. I wasn't in the mood to talk or make nice with people. I hadn't even been read my rights but I was being handcuffed while all of my possessions were being scoured by a dog. All I kept thinking about was the fact that they had no search warrant to go through my things.

"I have bad news. The dog is going crazy," a second Marshall came walking in unannounced.

The Marshall that had handcuffed me spoke as he reached for my ID.

He grabbed it from the counter where he had my wallet and cash laid out.

"Mr. Reid, Mr. Reid," he muttered, somberly.

The female Marshall observing us all this time instantly picked up her camera.

"Rolling!" she stated, pointing the camera on the two main characters.

I was the Villain and Mr. Scott the Knight in Shining Armor. I would have imagined that if I was getting arrested, I would be shocked and out of my mind. For some strange reason, though, a sense of calm washed over me. Was I in shock? Was I numb? Was I dreaming? Well, I know I wasn't dreaming, but as for the rest, I guess I'll never really know. My mind was rather still and focused. I watched them talk amongst themselves, almost as if I were invisible.

"So, Mr. Reid, as you already might have suspected, you're under arrest," the Marshall explained.

He then proceeded to read me my Rights.

So, I guess this is it, I thought to myself. The end of the rope, my mother would say. That's what I get for following this path. Look where I had ended up. Arizona, all the way in Arizona. I kept punishing myself even after making so many mistakes. Now, I had made the biggest mistake of them all that was not going to be easily fixed.

"So, your accomplice, Mr. Murray is saying that this is all yours," the Marshall stated, holding a recorder up toward my mouth.

"I guess it's all mine then if that's what he told you," I replied.

I stared at the Marshall to insinuate that his intimidation tactics did not work with me. If he was looking for me to say something about Murray, I guess he didn't get what he wanted to hear.

"So, you did all of this by yourself? All this weight is yours? You're saying Mr. Murray didn't know you had all of this in the car, even though he was the one that was driving?" he asked firmly again and again.

"No sir, he had no idea. I'm not familiar with the area so I asked him to drive me on an errand," I countered.

Badgering the witness, Your Honor, would have been the response of a lawyer if it were an episode of Law and Order. He labored on, repeating the same questions but kept getting the same answer.

"If that's the case, then I'll let Mr. Murray go," he stated, clicking his recorder to an Off position.

Soon after the Marshall left the room, Murray was escorted past the room that I was being held. I was surrounded by glass on all sides, allowing us both a clear view of each other as he walked by. Murray nodded his head as the Marshall followed, flanked by officers on either side. They went to the car and got his luggage. I prayed that he would take my luggage also and pretend it was his. My belongings were inside and I feared the Marshalls wouldn't return them to me. It wasn't anything illegal, just a bunch of clothes and cell phones I had just bought.

The tall Caucasian investigator that had initiated my stop came back into the room once again.

"Well, Mr. Reid, we have to take a ride. If you can behave, you can ride with me. Otherwise, you can take a ride in the cruiser," he explained.

"Whatever you want to do, sir. It's not like I have a real choice in the matter," I replied, in a slightly sarcastic tone.

"Ok, then," he said as he helped me up and cuffed my hand in the front, instead of behind my back. The female Marshall complimented my outfit and I managed to crack a smile as I thanked her.

Exiting the building, I felt like a vampire walking out into the bright sun. It was scorching my face. It felt like I walked into a pizza oven set to 500 degrees. The heat was seemingly unbearable. All of my days here had been spent in a hotel room that was perfectly cooled by the gentle breeze of the air conditioner. It hadn't registered what the heat truly felt like in Arizona until today. The Marshall opened the door to his F-150 truck and watched closely as I hopped up and bounced into the *passenger seat. A new surge of calmness prevailed over my body. I was completely relaxed. Exhausted rather from pulling a drug-dealer all-nighter. Believe it or not, as the Marshall drove off into the hot Arizona desert, I fell asleep with cuffs on my hands. I opened my eyes momentarily and saw white lines on the pavement disappearing under his truck. He drove on and I unconsciously fell asleep. The rhythm of the van was steady and complimented my tiredness. I obliged and took advantage of the unsavory moment and destination where I was headed.*

The truck skidded to a halt and dreams quickly shifted to a nightmare of a reality. A big steel reinforced door marked 'PPD' stood in front of me. I was sure this was some type of Federal building. It was huge and there were brand new cars everywhere with 'evidence' marked on most of them. The car that I had rented was on a tow truck that pulled in right behind us.

"Mr. Reid, we have arrived," the Marshall confirmed.

Where, I still don't know, but at least we were here.

"Where is this?" I asked in a low tone.

I rubbed my eyes and spun around 180 degrees to see my entire view. There were more cars and trucks tucked away in the back and spiraled up a parking garage. Motorcycles were chained together on the farthest wall, shielding the compound from the outside world. The door was flung open and the Marshall exited his vehicle, yet I had not realized he did.

"Let's go," he commanded opening the door of the van. I stepped out of the truck, my eyes darting from one thing to the next, scanning the horizon and taking in all that I could see. The Marshall's eyes were transfixed on my black socks and shoes. I almost felt like asking if he wanted to check inside of them or if he was simply taking fashion notes!

As we entered the building, he got on his radio and a second door buzzed open. The powerful steel door slowly slid to the right, allowing us to enter inside. Upon entering, I noticed there was absolutely nothing except for a computer sitting on a desk, a chair and big oversized cinder blocks that were used in the construction of the walls. The Marshall pulled the chair out and motioned me to sit. He asked for my date of birth, my name, and other pertinent information. Nothing seemed to elicit a reaction from him until he asked me where I was born and I replied, "Jamaica."

"You fucking Jamaicans," he exclaimed furrowing his eyebrows as he gathered his thoughts. "Why is it that you're telling me you're moving all this weight by yourself, and at such a young age?" he said, frustrated by my antics.

"I told you, it's all mine. I think that's enough, Sir," I said with a hint of sarcasm. "When will I be able to make my phone call? I'm not really planning on staying here longer than I have to," I firmly stated, reaffirming the fact that we were not seeing eye to eye.

The Marshall was less than impressed by my comment, forcing him to call in backup. Two uniformed officers came and escorted me to a cell. The bench was made out of concrete and was understandably cold and uncomfortable. I guess my sarcasm must have pissed him off. Maybe he didn't have the best relationship with Jamaicans. Maybe it was a little bit of both, or he was just an asshole that wanted to make a point of who was in charge. I spent two hours torturing myself as I lay on a freezing concrete bench. Finally, the bars slid open and the Marshall called my name. "Round 2," I thought to myself as I was ushered back into his little office.

Upon meeting with the Marshall again, I was booked, questioned some more, my picture was taken, and I was fingerprinted.

"Have you ever been arrested before?" he asked.

"No, sir," I replied tersely.

"Ok," he said, "go back into the cell."

As I turned and walked away, the door slammed behind me before I even had a chance to sit down. My only source of familiarity quickly became a damned cold bench. Once back in the cell, I was left alone with my thoughts. The journey had begun without me even knowing it.

Fighting Just to Dream

It had been a little over a week since Shawn had left. My cell was now the party room. YG, of course, was the most frequent guest. He had calmed down a notch and was slightly more level-headed in conversations. He too, would bring up Shawn in random conversations from time to time. He had been promised for days now that his bond would be paid, yet he was still here. I was so mad that I cursed his family and friends for leaving him in here. After much conversation, I was given a different perspective of his situation. He shed some light on the fact that even though he's here, his family and friends still have their lives to live. They have bills and expenses to pay. They all looked to him to help so now that he is away, no one was even somewhat capable of pulling things together. To him, it wasn't their responsibility to get him out this situation anyways.

I was proud of him. He was finally getting what I was telling him. Responsible people never shift blame to become a victim. A matter of fact, I only knew that because I had done it myself. A part of being imprisoned and becoming a man was to start taking responsibility for our actions and ultimately accepting the punishment that we were given. I further explained to him that he should stop thinking that everyone was just like him. He would comment that his best friend didn't even do a whole day in jail before he had gone and bonded him out. Now he was here and stuck because of seven hundred and fifty dollars. He finally started to grasp the concept that having expectations often sets you up to be let down. All he could do in this situation was to learn from it and make every change necessary to ensure that he would never set foot back in this hell.

Most inmates walked between the line of confines wearing a mask. This was not a literal mask, but rather a façade as they portrayed themselves as tough guys, gangsters, killers, drug dealers, and gang bangers. Each one believed that they were the most hardened criminal to ever enter Durango Jail. As for me, I didn't want to be here nor did I plan on staying, so I cared less what people thought of me. I wanted out at the earliest date. I spoke freely on being a human versus their racial segregated system. I openly showed feelings and emotion and consciously chose not to act as if I was constructed of iron and screws. To me, jail was far more challenging on a mental level, rather than a physical one.

My stature and respect for myself by not doing drugs or joking around drinking hooch was enough to scare off most. I held positive conversations with anyone that felt comfortable talking with me. I made sure these conversations were always something of substance, as shooting-the-air struck me as a waste of time and time was my most valuable commodity. A matter of fact, I had always heard time is money. I wouldn't waste money, so why would I choose to waste time? I was always told that if you invest time wisely, it would bring you dividends in return.

YG began to follow in my footsteps. He would come to my cell to discuss my philosophy on having a constructive thought process. He decided he was going to work on his vocabulary and be more positive. I was proud of him, but I also explained that he needed patience and understanding as all good things in life take time. While my advice was wise, it was not always easy to live by.

It wasn't mid-day and I was already in a heated conversation with my girlfriend.

"You need to be a man. You need to start respecting me like I respect you," she yelled over the phone.

I had done so much wrong and yet, she was still by my side. I listened as she explained what she had been going through since my physical departure. For some reason, the words she said about being a man hit me the hardest. A man must both give and receive respect. I had never before in my life been challenged on such an extreme mental level. The challenge I faced being in county jail awaiting sentencing was one of endurance. Her question challenged me to grow and evolve to become a better man. Four years of accounting classes in college hadn't challenged me like this question did. As far as school was concerned, it was always easy for me. Plus, there were always teachers to help when it got rough. Sometimes, the answers were even right there for you or in the back of the book. Being a man though, that meant walking the walk and talking the talk. Upon much time and introspection, I realized that all this time I had been using a cheat sheet to being a man. Cheat sheets are deceptive though. They give you answers, but it doesn't always mean it's the right answer. Money had always been the complicating factor in my life. I finally realized that having enough money allowed you to be "the man," but it certainly didn't always mean that you were "a man."

It was time for a change. Like the Renaissance Era, it would be a rebirth of my new attitude toward life. I embarked on this new mental voyage, understanding that my thought process had to change, as actions are the end results of your thoughts. This uncomfortable butterfly, a cramp-like feeling in the pit of my stomach, would become my driving force. I knew this was going to be tough. Understanding the dream is easy. Taking the journey step by step was a whole different story. But I welcomed the challenge as I knew my only chance at success laid within making these changes. Challenges would not deter my journey but only add substance to my experience. With my perceptions changed, my outlook changed, and my future changed, I could create a whole new me.

"Rude Boy, wha gwan," YG entered the room yelling.

I had gotten deep in my meditation and had quickly traveled far, far away.

"What's up, my brother," I responded, taking a few seconds to gather my thoughts. "You good?" I asked him curiously, as I could tell that he had something on his mind.

"I just got indicted," he told me, shrugging his shoulders and hanging his head.

YG embodied the defeat that an athlete felt as when he lost the game from a buzzer beater. His face grew pale as he further explained.

"Rude Boy, this is my first arrest and they want to send me to prison."

He shook his head.

"Welcome to my world," I agreed in disbelief. "Being indicted only means the grand jury found enough evidence to take you to court," I explained to YG.

I only knew because my lawyer had explained it to me eight months prior.

"Oh," he quietly muttered, drifting off into a thought. With so much heartache and devastation going on in here, it was no wonder that everyone walked around on egg shells every day. "What else did your paperwork say?" I further inquired.

"It said that bitch ass snitched on me. Oh, and they have my fingerprint on the jewelry box. All that shit was fake too. I can't believe I'm in jail for eight dollars," he ended.

He continued to curse and verbally deconstruct himself as he rambled on, lost in his own thoughts. YG had tried to pawn a box of Rolex watches, but they had turned out to be fake. Now his fate lay in the hands of a judge. The streets, the lifestyle, I questioned it all. The bad days outweigh the good days, so how do you win in the game? You become wealthy yet still live in fear that you will be robbed. A simple drug transaction can turn into a homicide at the drop of a dime. "The boys," or law enforcement, were constantly trailing you and watching for you to take one misstep. The game, or so it's called, was losing a player. As intriguing as it may sound to find somebody that may lessen your expenses, thus raising your profit, my eyes had been opened. The game seemed petty in the grand scheme of the journey of life. I had lost interest.

I was sure that I would be granted probation. I had absolutely zero criminal background and had been told by numerous people that my character reference letters written to the judge on my behalf were some of the most consistent and commendable that they had seen. My lawyer had cooked up a scheme to get me out of that. I was fearful for my life; he requested a free talk then denied it but presented the request to the judge. My soccer coaches, teammates, University professors, family, extended family and even the Dean of my University had all taken the time to write to the judge, illustrating my background, my worth, and my potential for the future. I wanted the second chance and I wanted to make the greatest use of it if it was given to me.

My preparation included much brainstorming so that I could be sure to make my next move my best move. To say that it would be easy would be as if to still think the world was flat. The feeling that I got from selling drugs was entirely more powerful than the drugs themselves. Naturally, withdrawals would be a part of my recovery process. Setting attainable long term and short-term goals would be a crucial aspect of my recovery journey and I was fully committed to not only reaching but also exceeding every single one of those goals along the way.

The defeated look that I saw on Shawn's and other inmates as they headed off to prison was a reminder of the fate that I, myself, may incur. If I was going to be served the same fate, as God was to have it, then I prayed to make the best and most effective use of any time that I was given. I made up my mind that time would serve me rather than vice versa. I believed in a quote that I thought of everyday that went as follows, "The mind in itself can create a heaven out of hell or a hell out of heaven." Success was the only result that I would entertain. I believed in myself and if there was one thing I knew, it was that I would always find a way.

Three weeks down, one week to go until my sentencing. More inmates came and went. Fights continued and increased in frequency during the weekend, as the normal routine would suggest.

"What's good Rude Boy," YG asked.

"Nothing, my brother. Just chilling as usual," I answered.

"Shit, you don't come out anymore. These dudes out here are messing with this new Wood. He believes anything that you tell him. They got him so scared, telling him that he's got to get smashed by the Woods as a welcome to the pod. Some dude even told him he's got to be his bitch," YG laughed hysterically, slapping his hand on the mirror, which made a loud thumping noise. "Come play some spades with me," he begged.

The noise seemed to echo in my cell for seconds. I rolled over and finally pulled myself to sit up. I had no interest in seeing who this kid was, but I decided that a break from my cell might be alright after all.

"Who are we going to play?" I inquired, grabbing the bar of the top bunk to help myself up.

Keyes had moved out of my cell to the tents for work release. His bunk was now empty. Curtis still remained as my cellmate, although I wish that was not the case as his flatulence had become unbearable. He showed me the true meaning of silent but deadly! You would be sleeping and suddenly the torture drifting through the air would suffocate your nostrils until you had no choice but to jostle awake. The best part was that he wouldn't have a clue that he had aerated the cell and wreaked havoc on everybody around him. YG screamed, "Damn brother!" YG yelled. "Why you do me like that?" he asked, covering his face with the towel he had been wearing around his shoulders. "Let's get out of here. That's my celly. He just takes all those pills, sleeps, and farts all day and he

Fighting Just to Dream

doesn't even smell himself. He's been killing me ever since I got here, bro," I laughed, covering my nose before the smell caught me once more. I hurried out of my cell and didn't breathe again until I reached the card table.

We played a few games with the Pisas. They always cheated by speaking Spanish to each other. Today, they had to switch up their scheme because they knew I had picked up a bit of their Spanish.

"Ta ta ta dah," the Pisas yelled in the form of a song.

"Hey," I shouted. "Stop with your little cheating games!" Everyone laughed as one of the Pisas translated to his friend what I had just said. They laughed again.

"He asked how you knew he was cheating," his friend asked me, translating what the Pisa had said to him in Spanish.

"I don't know but every time he does that shit, he's cutting, so it has to be a sign! And you always come back with the same suit!" I exclaimed slapping my cards as I hit his suit but with a higher spade.

I had gotten better at spades but hadn't played in a while. Just wasn't interested. YG laughed and grabbed the cards. He looked at his hand and signaled for me to come back with the same suit. I was certainly no master at this game, but I felt like one of the best today. I had learned how to play from YG and Shawn. It was just another way to pass the time for me.

"Look at you, Rude Boy! You're calling people out now? You're finally learning how to play!" YG excitedly shouted, slapping his card on the table and taking the book.

"Step your game up! I'm about to take the belt from London and Thatcher," I said loudly, directing my voice toward London and Thatcher's cell.

It didn't take long for me to get a reply.

"Jamaica! Is that you calling us out?! We are the champions. We are the spades champions!" Thatcher repeated over and over in his little comedian-esque voice.

"Hell, yea,"YG jumped in without even giving me a chance to reply. "We ain't scared. Put that belt London built up and get it taken," he ended.

London had continuously paraded around the pod with his so-called spades belt looking for challengers, and at times even taking bets on the game. London came to his cell door and stretched. He turned around and reached for something, pulling his spades belt into sight and placing it around his waist.

"You challenging the spades champion, Jamaica?" he asked smirking. "YG, I'm not talking to you. You're not going to put no money up but I know that Jamaica will," he ended. Somehow, I couldn't turn down the bet after I had called them out.

"Three sodas, right now," I quickly replied adding a sudden twist. "YG and Pisa versus you and Thatcher."

The pod was excited as everyone had waited a very long time for the day that the spades belt would leave the Whitehouse. London and Thatcher's cell had been aptly named the Whitehouse because only two inmates occupied it. Both were Woods, hence the name.

"No, you have to play. You can't sub Pisa into this," Thatcher joined the conversation, full of his Texas drawl.

"I'm putting up the money. What, are you guys scared to lose, your belt?" I responded, challenging them to further incite a rivalry to increase the bet.

I asked YG to get three sodas from under my bed to show them that I was serious. I might lose my sodas but for once, the mood seemed to lighten with the prospects of a friendly yet competitive game of Spades. Everyone gathered around the table as the game began. The rules were set and neither party could back out now. The cards where shuffled and one was picked from the deck by each party to see who pulled the highest card. YG drew the guaranteed joker and slapped it on the table, blowing underneath it to make it jump. It made the card seem like it was dancing.

The game began and ended in the first hand with YG and Pisa getting wheels and setting London and Thatcher. Thatcher yelled at the top of his voice, "Bullshit, YG stacked the cards!" "That's crazy!" YG replied. "London cut the cards so blame your partner," he ended.

London appeared defeated, finding no excuse for his loss. The only words he could mutter were, "Run it back, anybody could win a game with a first hand set." YG opened up one of the sodas and handed the extra bottle to his teammate and toasted. He took a sip and smiled as the taste hit his pallet.

"Thanks for the sodas," he laughed. "Rude Boy, pop a bottle," he commanded as he continued to crack up.

London's pale color changed to red, the color of a well-cooked Maine lobster.

"Don't worry, London. I'll let you keep your belt. These sodas are way better anyways," YG taunted him.

The Woods weren't too happy with the display of competition that their fellow brothers had participated in. Nevertheless, London had a point. Best out of two should have always been the case but that wasn't in the agreement when they began to play.

YG grabbed on to me, barely able to stand as he buckled to his knees in mocking laughter. He handed me the three sodas that I had put up as collateral and then placed his arm around my shoulder. He held on to the extra soda with a tight grasp.

"Easy money, Rude Boy, easy money. I felt like I just strong arm robbed these White boys."

He barely overcame his laughter to mutter the few words. He had beat the champions and earned their belt. In his final display, he even let them keep the belt that he had earned, which only added insult to injury!

"Lock down! Everyone to their bunk spaces! Lock down," the officer shouted over the monitor.

It wasn't lockdown time so either something had happened or they were going to do searches. Everyone looked puzzled as they haphazardly retreated to their cells. Law enforcement had their codes and prisoners had their own codes as well. It could be anything from abiding by the code of silence when questioned, to whistling or somehow alerting other inmates of a cop who was entering the pod. Everyone was on high alert. The pods that had direct view to The Bubble where the guards stayed kept watch for other inmates as well. It was incredible how a pod could work together when it came to outwitting the cops. On just any regular day though, it was every race for themselves and a "kill or be killed" world.

The inmates screamed out alert after alert to let the pod know that the guards were on their way. The door buzzed and stopped, then continued to buzz again. The guard entered the pod and walked by everyone's cell, peeking inside and stopping momentarily to check others with more scrutiny. One by one he chose specific inmates and took them outside. He chose Africa, Liberia, Josh and the Wood that everyone had been teasing a while back. Everyone stood in the entry-way of their cells to try and see to get an understanding of what was going on. One by one, they were all taken out of sight and eventually returned again. Inevitably, everyone returned except for Liberia and the new Wood. Assumptions flew through the pod from cell to cell, word spreading quicker than wildfire.

Unfortunately, there was some truth to the rumors that we heard that day. YG, even though we were on lockdown, slid into our cell and sat down curled up on the floor. His escaped attempt from his room was one that exhausted him to the point that he was breathing heavily.

"Rude Boy, you're right my brother. Damn! "he exclaimed. "I never thought that kid would snitch though. Everyone was making jokes and thought the whole thing was funny. Poor Africa," he said, shaking his head from side to side.

"Africa or Liberia,"I asked him, trying to put the pieces of the puzzle together. "The story I heard from my neighbor was that Liberia is the villain rather than Africa?" I asked confused by the set of events that had taken place.

"Oh, no Africa I mean," YG barely got through speaking before I remembered him saying that someone had snitched.

"Who snitched?" I asked.

Whether in jail or on the streets, this was a big no-no. As I understand how it works in Durango, snitching meant getting smashed and it was not uncommon to lose your life in the process.

"Fat Boy snitched on Africa. He said Africa threatened him and that he feared for his life. Now Africa has an extra charge! They are sending him back to 4th Avenue for processing right now. Damn, we were just playing around with the kid though," he ended, sitting down on the foot of my bed.

Curtis lay down on his bed, somehow without ever inquiring about the conversation. It seemed that we were alone until his voice caused us to acknowledge that he was there and accounted for.

"I told them to stop messing around with that boy. That boy clearly looked scared. Everything might be fun and games, but when shit hit the fan, is it though? That boy knows nothing about jail. Of course, he is thinking y'all are serious," he explained his eyes still closed.

"He didn't have to snitch on nobody," YG explained in a very blunt voice. "Nobody told him to come to jail. He should have known we was only playing with him."

"Yo, my brother," I exclaimed, taking his full attention away from his thoughts. "That's why I told you to leave the dude alone. He's clearly not all there so I would imagine it wouldn't be hard for him to believe everything that you told him. No sane person can be so gullible. I saw it on his face the minute you showed him to me. Just count your blessings and be glad that he didn't catch you up in all the drama. I hope you learn from this and understand that a simple joke to you can turn into a whole separate charge. Be thankful and take it as a lesson."

He sat holding the iron supporting the bed's frame.

Damn! Africa was cool and now he had another headache on top of the rest of the problems he was already facing. This place is already so negative and to add more might just make it all unbearable. I couldn't imagine what he must have been going through. I'd be beating myself up for even joking around with the Wood. As a man, you have to make choices in life and you have the right to be good or to be bad. Don't make a choice as a man and snitch on someone else in hopes of receiving a handout for yourself. If you are man enough to make decisions then deal with those consequences as a man as well. If I were a law enforcement agent, I would not respect a snitch. If you cannot manage to accomplish a particular goal, find a way to do it or create one yourself. Nothing attempted, is nothing achieved. To *try* is for suckers.

For the remainder of the day, our pod remained locked down. The lieutenant had placed the pod on 24-hour restriction because too many inmates had rolled-up. He also added that if we didn't figure out the problem then it would turn into a 48-hour restriction. I laughed to myself. I guess the inmates are the ones who run this place after all. The sense in the air was dark and thick. The structure of alliance had been reshuffled. I remained in my cell and when I became tired of laying on the bunk, I played cards with my cellmates while sitting on the floor. Some played chess while others read. It was the first time I'd seen some of these guys pick up a book. They read anything they could get their hands on. This had definitely been the longest day spent at Durango in my short tenure here. Inmates got so bored that they shouted in their cells as if their lives depended on it. Some banged on their windows and sang out into the pod. I felt I was living in an insane asylum.

Much to everyone's surprise, a talent was discovered that day. Cali, a Kinfolk, stood about six feet tall, 260 pounds, with a huge bald spot in the middle of his head. He hadn't spoken much since he had been here. He stayed to himself and came out his cell only to watch television which was constantly stuck on the food channel. He often attended bible study but most often he would just hang out on his bed. Today, his name was about to be changed. As the chaos continued, we heard a beautiful melody appear out of nowhere. This instantly lifted the spirits of the entire pod causing the noises of madness to disintegrate and disappear. The inmates fell quiet suddenly as our ears listened keenly. His song had a beautiful relaxing melody that allowed light to shine through the darkness. He sang from the depths of his heart as he went from one note to the next. He finally paused for a second, and everyone clapped and whistled. Some even gave him a standing ovation. The mood of the pod had become entirely different. It was the most relaxed that I had ever seen it. He continued to sing various songs and said a few words before he decided to stop because his voice grew raspy. He prayed for the pod and we gave him his new name, 'Radio'.

Radio's story was so unbelievable that you couldn't help but feel sorry for him. He was in jail because he didn't pay child support to himself. Yes, to himself. The system had failed him in more ways than one. How can something like this happen to a law-abiding citizen and still yet not rectified? 'Only in this state' I thought to myself. He was going to court for almost a year now about his child support issue. His children had previously lived with his ex-wife during their separation. Upon finalizing their divorce, the children came to live with him and he asked the court to remove his conditions to pay child support. Now because of his new arrangement with his wife, the courts wanted the wife to pay him child support but he declined the offer.

Well, the State had a different idea. Since he didn't want to accept money from his ex-wife, he now had to pay himself child support because they went back to the old condition of his previous contract. He was literally in jail for not paying himself child support. No matter how much he fought and how much support he had, it was as if the state was naturally against him. He couldn't understand how a system could treat its people in such a manner. The icing on the cake was he owed himself child support and the courts decided to give him a couple days in jail as recompense. They cared nothing about his kids whom he had to make arrangements for being locked up. In addition to losing a month of his life, his daughter had been raped since he was gone and he blamed himself for not being there to protect her. He was very intelligent and articulate. He was very well mannered and had graduated from UCLA. Radio had previously worked as a CPA for a local Fortune 500 company but he didn't know if he would still have a job when he was released.

"As a black man living in Arizona, your voice is not heard in the courts in this state. It really is the Wild-Wild West out here. First, you are put in jail, and then you must prove your innocence," Radio would fiercely explain.

He cursed the courts for failing his family. He was consumed with anger when he spoke of his story, but when he sang, he was at peace. It was heartbreaking to watch a grown man experience so much tragedy, but when he sang, it was beautiful and therapeutic. He believed very strongly in seeing the silver lining in everything and kept his faith strong.

"It is all God's plan," he'd proclaim assuredly after he finished recounting his hardship. Only God knows what is to come for Radio, but I know one thing for sure: there must be some good to come for him after this dark road, as all that pain and anger that bellowed out of his vocal cords would never be able to produce such a moving melody otherwise.

"35 Bed 2! 35 Bed 2!" the monitor rang out.

The bed space had never been called over the monitor before today.

"Rude Boy, it's you," YG came tapping on my bed.

"35 bed 2, legal visit. Bring your ID with you," the officer ordered.

"My lawyer must be here to see me," I said, a bit rushed, as I suddenly felt slightly uneasy.

"Good luck, my brother," YG wished as the door buzzed for me to push it open.

I sat in the middle of the building, waiting on a warm bench. The officer handed me a visitation slip and handcuffed my wrist and ankles. He brought out two other inmates from two separate blocks then escorted us to the visitation building. Entering the visitation room, I was placed into a holding tank until the officer called my name, then brought me into a private room where I sat down with my lawyer. It was the typical jail visitation room: iron bench paired with aluminum tables so shine that I could see my own reflection. I hadn't seen or used a mirror in weeks, not since I got to County at least. I tried not to look down at it. I didn't want to see my reflection.

Mr. Brooks. He was tall and frail. Jewish, his beard unevenly shaved and his nose hairs were so long I'm sure it could be braided. His shoulders were square but they didn't represent strength. His clothes were oftentimes stained from coffee spills and they always seemed a bit wrinkled. His briefcase told the story of how used it had been. Worn down from its usage. His personal office, however, was spotless. Regardless, he was my lawyer. I had met him through some type of mystical endeavor. He showed up to Maricopa County Jail just before I had to go to court. He was my knight in shining armor. Maybe he just went through the docket when I was brought into county my first time and saw I had no lawyer. Whatever the case was, he was my lawyer now. Actually, he had been for the past nine months. Expensive too at that. After all, he was a Jewish lawyer and boasted of his connections. His assistant wasn't here today. He was another character.

Inside the room, a beautiful blonde Caucasian woman sat facing me. She was professionally dressed in a white long-sleeved blouse, black pencil skirt that rested slightly above her knees and wearing stiletto heels. She sat with her legs crossed as she unpacked her laptop, in addition to a file jacket. She was very sexy, yet professional, even when she picked up her reading glasses and slipped them on, running them through her hair. She flicked the excess hair behind her shoulder and looked up. My eyes met hers.

"Hello, good afternoon, Mr. Reid. Pleased to meet you."

I stretched out my still cuffed hand to shake hers. I stared, unable to utter a word.

"Nice to meet you, Mr. Reid. I am Sarah and I am here to interview you. I work with Arizona Pre-Trial Service," she explained. I sighed in relief.

Miss Sarah had been the only other person that I had met that works for this state that had not tried to intimidate me or to bully me around because I was a prisoner.

"Mr. Reid, how are you doing?" Mr. Brooks asked. He was still unsettled grasping paper and pen while flipping through his briefcase. "Not too bad under the circumstances, Sir," I replied. Neither of us made eye contact. I was fixed on the smell of a woman. Oh man, perfume. The fragrance was dominating my senses.

"Excuse me, Sarah. Do you mind if I have a few seconds outside with my client? It will only take two minutes," he explained. "That's fine, Mr. Brooks. As long as I can be done before my next appointment, then I don't mind," she replied.

I liked it when my lawyer took control of my court proceedings and today, he had continued to impress me. We spoke briefly outside. He explained that if any unrelated questions were asked, he would decline the questions, as they were only there to talk about those relevant to the case.

The meeting began as soon as I walked in to the room. I saw my arrest photo on the table. I glanced at the photo and joked, "Wow, I guess the photographer didn't do me any justice!" Sarah and Mr. Brooks both chuckled and the mood in the room seemed to lighten. She asked me question after question about my life, covering all topics from my childhood through the present day. She asked me numerous questions about my education and my work history but told me that she was able to skip the criminal background questions as I had none. I ended the meeting with a few last words for her after she had told me that her portion of the meeting was through.

"Ms., I just want to be reinstated back into society. I had been a positive contributing member of society for most of my life. I made a mistake that I deeply regret and will for a long time to come, but at some point, I hope to use this very story to help others. I am a better man because of the punishment that I have been given. I have accepted my responsibility for my actions as a man should. Now, I have my entire family ready to assist me in all avenues. I have friends and officials in my community that have reached out and vying for my release to right my wrongs. I have my son to nurture so he can become a better man than I am and never make the mistake I made. If reinstated and given probation, I am 100% certain that I will not let anyone down, not even myself."

I ended the meeting teary-eyed.

Every word that I said was from my core. I thought about my loved ones that I hadn't seen in what felt like forever.

"Mr. Reid, I recommend," she stopped typing on her computer, paused for what seemed to be an eternity, and fixed her glasses. She continued, "I recommend that you are given probation, after reviewing all of the details of your case. Truthfully, I don't see why you are being sent to prison when this is your first offense. I will send this recommendation to the judge and to the prosecutor's office. Remember that this is just a recommendation. Ultimately, it is up to the judge and the prosecutor to make the final call. I wish you nothing but the best. Mr. Reid, I believe in you. Now, start believing in you and don't let yourself down."

She paused and took her glasses off.

"I must say that I am astonished that a smart, intelligent young man like yourself would get drawn into something like selling drugs."

She shook her head.

As she closed her computer and stood, she ran her finger through her hair and placed it behind her ear. She walked to the door, opened it, and looked back before stepping out.

"Mr. Reid, there are not many cases that I have reviewed that have struck me like yours. You have the most outstanding character reference letters that I've ever seen. It's unfortunate the situation you are in. Truly unfortunate," she ended, opening the door and stepping away.

"Mr. Reid, job well done to you. You handled that well. This is a step in the right direction. I hope the prosecutor comes to his senses after reading this Pre-Trial Services recommendation. Understand that nothing is set in stone, so don't get your hopes up too much, but we are definitely on the right track," Mr. Brooks advised.

We shook hands and parted ways. In seven days, my fate would be sealed in front of the judge. All I could do was to hope and pray that my fate would send me home to my family. Mr. Brooks and Mr. Chambers, his assistant, were geniuses. They were out of the box thinkers that created avenues that I hadn't dreamt of possible. Well, Mr. Chambers seemed to be a bit sketchy. Something about him was off. He was always so arrogant. As Mr. Brooks' assistant he'd pick me up from the airport when I'd fly in for court. The whole entire car ride he'd talk about his women and his mansion that he owned.

Returning to the pod, I explained to YG what had happened. He was rolled over laughing when I told him about my joke at the beginning of the interview, but I was thankful I was able to break that ice. He could feel my excitement as I told him about the positive atmosphere I felt in the meeting. Finally, it felt like something good was happening! The only thing was, I couldn't even share the good news with my girlfriend as the pod was locked down and the phones were turned off. Well, it must have been a sign from the universe. I spent the remainder of the day in my cell, rejoicing in my own optimism. My last words into the universe that night were, "This nightmare, too, shall pass."

The feeling from my interview was carried into the days ahead. I kept sending positive messages into the universe, hoping that I was going home Friday. I spoke to everyone as if I was out already that even YG started to pick up on it.

"Rude Boy, when you get out Friday, just bond me out. I know $750 is nothing to you," he requested.

I sure would have done it too. We had spoken more about his life, the path that he had taken to survive and what were his options moving forward. He explained that this wasn't the life that he wanted but a hungry stomach and mounting bills led him down this path of no return.

Sadly, I understood where he was coming from. Parts of my childhood were very tough being the youngest of three kids that all shared a one-room house in Jamaica. My mother was our primary caretaker and at times she was overwhelmed from her struggles. Life was definitely a rollercoaster that had its highs and its lows. One day we would be doing okay, the next we had no money to purchase basic necessities.

Living life as a drug dealer, I fed my conscience with the fact that I was helping my loved ones and that marijuana is a medicine, rather than a drug. Growing up in Jamaica, I was taught that marijuana was a part of nature and that it served medicinal purposes. I would never dream of selling something such as cocaine, but marijuana I say no problem with mass usage. Our American society, its laws and law enforcement saw it differently, however, as marijuana is considered to be a drug and a Schedule 1 gateway drug at that. I was seen as a deviant to society, a menace and it was commonly believed that I should be prosecuted as such.

"Life is all about choices. We don't make the right choices every day and sometimes, there is no guarantee that comes along with making that right choice. Because of that reasoning, we are more apt to take risks in hopes of receiving that wealthy payoff," I said to YG.

"I bet if you wanted the money to go bail out, you would find a way to get it. I'm not saying it's easy or that things happen overnight, because realistically they don't. I'm just saying that if you don't have it, make a way. First, we make the decision, then the decision makes you so make better decisions to create a better future for yourself."

I reached under my mattress and pulled a book out.

"After all of these lawyer expenses and after bonding out twice, I might be damn well near broke when I get out (as if I wasn't already). I refused to let that stop me though. When the going gets tough, it's only time to dig deeper and do what you have to do by using what you have. I write in this book every day and I brainstorm ways that I can add to my income legally. It's damn sure not going to happen overnight and I understand that. To keep it real with you though, there is nothing that is stopping you or me. We can start right here and right now and make a new way," I ended.

His eyes widened with hope as he listened to me earnestly.

"Win or lose, I'm taking a chance on myself in the right way. The worst that can happen is that I learn. I learn if I fail and I learn if I win."

YG and I smiled as we dapped each other, both feeling a renewed sense of purpose. One thing I knew to be true was that if you take care of the small things the big things would take care of themselves.

"My brother, one thing for sure is you have to change your mindset. I don't mean to repeat myself, but brother, just look at people that go to prison and come out doing the same thing. They go right back with more time and less money. They are wasting life and I don't want that for either of us. That belief that you carry to make it and then spend it, because you will get more back has got to go. Toss that shit out of the window. Make it, stack it, invest it, and make some more. I made all those dumb mistakes and every day that is something I wish I can change," I advised.

I could tell that he was as interested in learning more of what I was saying. Almost every one of us has the natural desire to become wealthier and more financially literate. Most of us, however, become a product of our environment. We let fear consume us because we don't want to be different from our peers. "What if being uncool made you wealthy," I asked YG, rhetorically.

"Fuck being cool. Rude Boy on some real shit. I'm stuck in jail right now," he said as he shook his head.

I knew I had his attention. I was looking for those words and I wanted him to say it to hear himself. Ultimately, he and I would part ways and I wouldn't be there to think for him so I wanted him to grasp the concept.

"All them licks I hit and all I did was ball out with my boys and paid a few bills."

YG gazed out the window as he spoke and sounded increasingly frustratedwith his past choices.

"The good thing about all of this is that you have time to slow down and realize who and what is really important to you. When I leave here, I guarantee you the lack of money is not going to drive me insane, but it is going to be my motivation. I am preparing mentally to use this experience as my stepping stone and allow it to motivate me. You should be thinking the same," I stated.

I wasn't the best person but I thought the least I could do was shed some light on our situation. Throughout this time, YG has always looked up to me as a big brother so I began to influence him positively rather than to lead him down a life of lie. My experience with both him and Shawn made me value their existence and wanted to have them both become successful and lifetime friends. I envisioned that someday we would be reminiscing over a dinner about our experiences shared at Durango. Maybe a reunion in the form of a vacation away from business life. We would not miss tasteless slop and mashed potatoes one bit.

"Rude Boy, I really don't want to go back to kicking doors down," YG said. "You know my boy died after he got shot in his stomach doing the same thing I keep doing just for a quick stack. He got a shot gun to the stomach, bro. His guts was hanging out. I use to wonder, 'what if I don't make it home to my mama?' Would I have helped her or just hurt her even more when she sacrifices just to be the bread-winner. I got shot once before and I don't care what people say, that shit hurt like hell. Man, I came from the projects but I definitely don't want to be there forever. Everyone looking at everyone, robbing each other and killing each other over nothing. My daughter died at 18 months because of this shitty ass life," YG paused for a second.

Throughout my time here, I never heard YG speak of having a daughter until now.

"That nigga is in LBJ and that's why I always use to try to pop off so I can go see that nigga. Rude Boy, I want them to move me over there to higher custody. They wanna let this dude off with probation for killing my daughter but indict me for fake Rolexes. Real talk, bro. I wanna bash dude head in. He shook my little girl and killed her."

YG wiped the tears that now ran down his cheeks. I felt so helpless hearing him speak. Nothing I could say was ever going to bring his little girl back. All that I could muster out was, "I feel for you, man. If somebody ever messed with my son, then it's all over. I get where you're coming from."

YG managed a forced smile.

"Man, my mama always told me I was going to be rich. Maybe I came here to meet you, Rude Boy. You definitely have me thinking about a lot of important things," YG said holding his hand up his chest as if he was holding his daughter.

His tears flowed as he continued to grieve.

The days flew by and my sentencing became my focal point. I kept imagining my options. I would either be going home or I would be going to the Pinto. Clearly, I would choose home in a heartbeat. What would the judge determine to be fit in my case though was more important. The judge had no way of knowing the growth that I had experienced in my short time here, so I made it my goal to speak on my own behalf at sentencing. I can only pray to God that I will come back in a better position than Shawn did. Either way, I was determined to speak in front of that judge. Failure was not an option for me. No matter what the verdict, I was going to make my story a successful one.

As usual, YG was in my cell all night long. He kept talking about anything and everything, trying to take my mind off of what was to come. Earlier in the day, I had written my little speech so I decided to read it for him.

> "Good morning, Your Honor," I paused and looked away from my script to visualize myself to be positioned in front of the judge. "I wanted to take this opportunity to apologize to the court, the State of Arizona, my friends and my family. I take full responsibility for my actions and I am committed to create a change in my life and others that I come in contact with. To commit to a great future using the lessons from my past. I am dedicated to righting my wrongs and I have always been a well-respected member of society and have more to contribute from the lessons life has continually taught me. I request to be given probation because I have no prior convictions and I have a two-year-old son to be a father to. If granted probation and allowed to return home to my family, I will not let myself fall back into a negative environment. I hope to be more than just a contributing member of society but a great role model for others to emulate. Thank you so much for allowing me to speak inside your court room. Your Honor, thank you and have a wonderful day!"

My speech was very sincere and from the heart. I know I wasn't perfect, but I know I was worth it.

"Brother! I feel everything you're saying. That is real shit. You're talking about everything you're doing right now too, so I dig that. I hope they let you out man, but before that, please write me one of these? Please, I'm begging you!" YG said, grabbing the paper and throwing it in the air jokingly. He was quite animated as we both laughed at his antics. "I really hope they give you probation though, bro. You're my big brother now, homie," YG ended picking up the paper off the floor. He left soon after, running around as he usually did.

Sleep was the last thing on my mind that night. I thought of the happiness that my girlfriend and my son would feel once they were finally able to see me again. It felt like I was free already. Reality crept in here and there as the positive thoughts were followed by 'what if's'. I tossed and turned all night long. I barely fell asleep before an officer stopped by my cell doing his rounds, knocked on my bunk. It was 3:00 am. Time for court yet court wouldn't be in session until 8:30 or 9:00 o'clock.

"Reid, you have court. Reid! Reid! Reid!" the officer's voice echoed over and over.

I woke up from my semi-conscious state and turned around feeling annoyed. I looked up at him in disbelief. I had barely closed my eyes; now I had to be up all day riding back and forth in buses shackled and in close quarters which inmates I didn't care to be around. It was time to get going and I instinctively jumped out of bed and grabbed my hygiene from under my mat. I felt as if I didn't even have time to rub my eyes before the monitors went off again calling all inmates to exit the pod for court. I was already starting to feel overwhelmed just thinking about the many hours it would take to travel a couple miles to court and back.

Today, I had critical matters to overcome. The magnitude of today was unparalleled and in order to perform my best, I had to feel good about myself. I took a quick shower even as the officers called my name and cell number over and over. A shower would always release some of the tensions I felt. I ran to my cell and got dressed, putting back on the very clothing I had been wearing all week, not to mention my shirt got ripped. My armpits, though fresh, were funky the instant I put the shirt back on. Jail hygiene was the worst but when you have no choice you still used it even if it didn't work. Nothing fitted perfect inside this place. Only if you were short and skinny like Shawn and YG were you'd be able to fit in some clothes. I peeked out of my cell and checked to see if the officer was looking or coming my way. He was walking from cell to cell checking ID tags. I slipped into the bathroom one more time to check the damage I had done to the shirt. My entire chest and armpit had suffered severe damages. I heard the recognizable pounding of the footsteps with jingling of the keys drawing near.

"Reid, you have five minutes to be fully dressed. Don't forget your ID. Be outside in five minutes. No later," he ended, trying to be blunt and stern.

The sound of the jostling keys slowly disappeared and I heard the buzz of the door then silence as the door slammed shut. I picked up my ID tag and slipped it over my wrist. I walked by YG's cell and peeked in to see what he was doing. He was covered up from head to toe like a mummy. He was fast asleep. I waved my hand under the camera. That was our nonverbal request to open the door to leave the pod. In the hall, a few inmates already sat waiting on benches. I noticed they all used their shirts as blankets to try and warm themselves up. The AC must have been set at freezing temperatures to further break us down. The cold air became unbearable. The floor and the walls were all ice-cold. I felt as if I was entering into the tundra. There was only one bench near a small table for all of us that was already occupied. I slipped past everyone and found myself a discarded mattress that was left in the corner. I sat down and made myself comfortable.

I hadn't been sitting for five minutes before a rush of inmates came pouring in. They were all housed in different pods but we all had court today. Some inmates would be going home today;

others would be going to prison and the remaining few would do this again at a later date. Going to court was a drawn-out and unnecessarily time-consuming ordeal. You were woken up anywhere from 2:00 to 3:00 am. You were gathered, strip-searched, and changed into stripes that were either entirely too big or too small. The officers chose what clothing to give you and made a mockery of everyone. After that, we simply sat and waited for four hours. After that point, you were finally loaded onto a bus with shackles around your hands and feet and delivered to court as cattle in the modern-day slave trade.

For now, we had to sit on the floor and wait for the entire process to unfold. I remained seated and an officer approached me inquiring if I believed I was special. He removed the mattress and screamed as he walked away.

"Nobody's allowed to sit there!" he stated, pushing his chest out. I smiled and stood up, standing over him for a few seconds. "Jamaica. Rude Boy!" exclaimed a familiar voice in the distance.

London was sitting in the group of inmates and recognized me from my little disturbance with the officer. He was smiling from cheek to cheek as if he was Mr. Kool-Aid himself.

"What's up, my brother?" I said shaking his hand.

Even though racial tensions ran rampant inside Durango, London and I had a cool relationship. This was definitely not the typical case between inmates. He sat down on the ground and I slid down to join him. The cold floor sent a chill up my spine instantly. We chatted the whole time about what had happened after his fight with the wrestler. The needless drama that ensued since his departure were many. He said he had denied everything about the fight but the wrestler told everything to the officers when he was asked his side of the story. There was no way he was coming back to Building 7. The officers had him spend two weeks in the hole and had the wrestler in a cell right next to him. They moved him to Building 3 two days ago. We made a deal to collect each other's debt as the wrestler owed me and a Wood named Alex, owed him. I sure was glad to see a familiar face. Time passed a little more easily as we got to catch up.

We sat on the floor and waited for our names to be called as inmates began to climb onto a parked bus outside. London and I were on the same bus. It was comforting to have him there but once inside, I put my game face on. I barely spoke. I was practicing my speech over and over again in my head. Out of nowhere, the inmate sitting next to me decided to break the silence.

"Court today, huh," he said, trying to engage in a conversation. "How long are you looking at?" he asked.

"Sorry my man, I'm not in the mood to talk this morning," I replied to him, speaking in a stern manner as my eyes stared straight ahead.

"How about them Yankees," he said.

I cracked a smile and laughed, shaking my head. 'What a question', I thought to myself. He turned his head and looked through the window, whispering under his breath, "Only trying to have a conversation." I didn't reply; I pretended I didn't hear him. My poker face was in full effect again and emerging successfully from this court appearance was the only thing on my mind.

We turned toward the courthouse and pulled to a stop. The buses took us underground, then we were separated in different holding tanks. London and I were together again.

"Yow, man, why you following me?" I jokingly asked.

"Hey, Jamaica, if I didn't have to be here I wouldn't, brother. Trust me. This the last place I want to be," he ended.

The morning evoked a tired, nostalgic feeling. Most inmates ended up giving in and laid toilet paper on the floor to sleep on. I refused to sink to that level. London and I sparked up a conversation every time that sleep threatened us. London eventually fell victim. In no time at all he started snoring. The only excitement of the morning came when the officer brought Lamo bags. Everyone was up in seconds to eat our first of two meals for the day. True to my routine, I gave my Lamo bag away for oranges.

Inside the holding tank, the only place to relieve yourself was a basin that was situated in the far corner. This basin was surrounded by inmates from every which way you looked. This only meant one thing and that was that eating was a no-no. An officer came and opened the door sometime around 8:00am, taking four of us out, including London. We all had to see the same judge that day. I don't know if this was just all a coincidence or if it was in God's plan to lighten the mood, but regardless of the reason, I was thankful to have London to talk to. Inside of the last tank, the inmate in front of me was uneasy.

"Rude Boy, he's high as hell right now. He's tweaking," London whispered.

I laughed out loud, breaking the silence surrounding us. No one could hear us but we saw civilians entering the courtroom. "That's crazy," I said.

I looked at the guy momentarily, just to see him twitching and biting his lip. His eyes were about to pop out of their sockets. 'This must be what meth does to people,' I thought to myself, grimacing at his bloodshot eyes.

"Reid, you're up for court," the Marshall said as he slid the key into the door and pulled it open. "Your lawyer would like to talk with you before you enter the courtroom," he continued, opening the door and revealing an empty room with a chair and a two-way window.

I sat by myself for a few minutes until my lawyer appeared, carrying what seemed to be a mountain of paperwork.

"Mr. Reid, unfortunately, I have bad news," he said somberly.

I immediately hung my head down, my spirit instantly broken. "The prosecutor still will not agree to grant you probation, even after the Pre-Trial Services recommendation. They want to give you the maximum of two and a half years in prison."

"So, no probation at all," I interrupted, setting the record straight for myself.

"No probation," he replied. "I will argue for the least amount of time, being one year, but there is never any guarantee," he ended, slipping me the paperwork, which reiterated what the prosecutor was asking for.

A part of me wanted to shatter the window in anger if I could and a part of me had already subconsciously prepared for that sort of outcome. At this point though, I didn't even know what to feel. Breathing felt unnatural.

The Marshall came back and escorted me into the courtroom. The first thing I did was to look into the back of the room for any familiar faces. Not recognizing anyone there, I stood next to my lawyer and looked straight at the judge. He held my life's freedom in the palm of his hand. He asked my name and date of birth and moved forward, speaking on the matter at hand.

"Mr. Reid, I have read your character letters, your Pretrial report and I also understand that you have signed your plea."

He stopped reading for a moment and turned a few pages before continuing.

"Does the Prosecution grant the defendant probation or does the State decline?" he asked, glancing at the well-dressed miniature stature of a man. This man was my worst enemy and he had all the power.

"The State declines to grant probation, Your Honor. If Mr. Reid chooses to pursue probation, then the State would be obligated to take him to trial," he ended. "Mr. Reid, do you have anything to say?" he asked while looking again in my direction.

I had been practicing my speech for days but even if I spoke, the prosecutor was never going to change his mind.

The judge spoke.

"Mr. Reid, I sentence you to 18 months to be served in the Arizona Department of Corrections."

My lawyer argued right away and fervently questioned why had I not been given the minimum of twelve months, as eighteen seemed extreme compared to probation. The judge wasted no time in arguing that he could have imposed two and a half years instead. My lawyer then requested that I be granted credit for time served while I was awaiting sentencing. Anything else that was spoken about was nothing but a blur to me. I was utterly defeated. I felt like I had the wind knocked out of me. Prison was set in stone now and that journey would have to take its natural course. My lawyer and his assistant both shook my hand, with sorrow in their eyes. We exited the courtroom and the Marshall escorted me into the small room to finish talking with my lawyer. He cursed the prosecutor as I listened. Tears rolled down my cheek, one after the other. Mr. Chambers, his assistant, was speechless. He was mad with Mr. Brooks and himself. I respected them both for all they had done but I had paid them a lot money for their services. Mr. Brooks did his best to reassure me that I'd be fine in prison.

Mr. Brooks, excused himself from the brief meeting and I was alone with Mr. Chambers. We spoke about life, about our mistakes, and not letting them define your remaining years. We spoke of legal business opportunities that we were both interested in and just of life itself. He had been in the Air Force, served on the police force, worked as a Marshall, and most recently operated as a bounty hunter. He owned and operated a bail bonds company and had previously worked in real estate. Come to find out, he had been on the wrong side of the law himself before as well. I believe I reminded him of himself, somehow. He always went the extra mile when it came to my case. I expressed my gratitude to him for guiding me throughout my court appearances and even for giving Mr. Brooks some motivation in settling my case in the most beneficial way possible.

"Mr. Reid, you'll be fine. I wish you nothing but the best."

He ended the conversation.

I went back to the holding tank and as it slowly filled up with inmates, I felt myself becoming more and more uneasy. I was suppressing my feelings of depression. Crying felt like it would ease the heavy load I felt, but I wouldn't allow it. My pride was everything to me. The court system would not enjoy such a victory. I talked myself into being tough both inside and out. I didn't speak at all until I reached back to Durango.

Entering into D7, the pod that held transitioning inmates who were coming and going from court, everything seemed so different than it had been before. I wasn't going to be here much longer. I would have three more days here at the most and then Alhambra would be my next stop. As the officer signaled for me to step forward, I peered into the pod to see YG frantically waving his arms over his head. He clearly was much more excited than I was. I instinctively shook my head from side to side and it appeared he understood my message. It wasn't a good day, or so I thought. The news was nothing like we both had hoped. He dropped his hands onto his head and grabbed hold of his hair and pulled it in disbelief.

"What pod are you in?" the officer asked.

"D pod," I said to the officer in The Bubble.

He was gazing at the inmates talking through the crevice in the door so I knocked on the glass to spark his attention. He was pissed and quickly buzzed the door open. It was the first time I was glad to be here. I just wanted a shower and a bed. I didn't care about food. YG pushed the door open. He looked more disappointed than I was at this point. I had had enough time to process the information but it was all still new to him.

"What's good, my brother," I said in a low tone.

"What happened?" he asked, anxiously twirling his fingers through his hair. He wanted to hear the whole story and I didn't want to speak. I sighed heavily as I sat down on my bed,

"Where do I even start?" I muttered. "This bitch ass prosecutor must have something to prove. Even the judge wanted to give me probation! The prosecutor insisted on the max of two and a half years and that's all he could focus on. He didn't care about none of the character reference letters or that I had no priors. Before I even got into court, he requested maximum sentence. The judge had to meet him halfway so he gave me 18 months in prison, so I guess I might just see Shawn soon," I ended staring aimlessly into the ground.

"Fuck that bitch ass, Rude Boy. Fuck him!" he exclaimed, passionately expressing his feelings the same way I felt.

The last thing I wanted was sympathy so I concluded the whole conversation about court and the time I was given.

"At least he didn't give me the max," I said as I brought the silence to an end.

I knew that it was all fresh but I needed to start viewing my sentence in a positive light.

I had to tell the story at least one more time as I began to talk to my girlfriend on the phone. Our conversation wasn't as I expected. She had been at the gym with her mom and didn't want to talk about it then. She asked me to call her back, so I waited until it was late in the afternoon. I knew she would be alone to talk then. As soon as she picked up the phone, I could already hear her crying. She managed to ask, "You're not coming home, huh?"

"No, babe. Not for another year at least. The judge gave me 18 months, but I'm a first-time offender so I won't do all of that time," I tried to explain.

I initially had to try and make the time lesser in my mind, but to her it was forever. The last thing I wanted to do was lie, but I wished I could ease her pain. She broke into a more terrifying cry and shouted, "You didn't even kiss me goodbye before you left! I love you, babe." She kept crying and muttered, "You'll be fine. I'm waiting for you." As she said that she bellowed a cry that broke my heart to pieces, knowing that I was the source of her pain. We spoke for what seemed to be hours.

After the 15 minutes ended, I called her right back as she requested. Our last phone conversation for the night had me in tears. Before walking away from the phones, I had to wipe my tears and blow my nose to compose myself as best as possible before entering into my cell. YG was sitting on my celly's bunk. He knew I had shed a few tears and his eyes turned red. He felt the pain in the air and wanted to cry himself too. I laughed at him but he didn't appreciate the fact that I noticed his emotion.

"I thought gangsters don't cry! You better not be crying. I already let all that shit out!" I laughed.

He was still not amused. I was only trying to cover up my true feelings to lighten the mood because I didn't want to see any more people hurting over a journey that I would now inevitably be embarking on. I looked up into the top bunk and continued to speak while avoiding eye contact with YG.

"The worst part about this is," I paused looking at the graffiti drawing of a bulldog at the bottom of the bunk. "I'd give anything to be home with my girlfriend and son right now. They are affected by this as much, if not more, than I am." I paused again as I realized that I was unable to stop the single tear that ran down my cheek as my voice cracked. "This too shall pass," I said.

YG was speechless, his overwhelming emotion had slowed him

down today for sure. We just sat there in silence with minds so busy that the noise was deafening.

Later that night following count, I showered and took refuge in my bed. I thought of everything dear and important to me until I fell asleep only from sheer mental and physical exhaustion. The next few days passed in an anxiety-riddled blur as I struggled to comprehend what the future held. The journey that was to come had my imagination running rampant. What was prison like? Would I be okay? The stories my father had told me did not seem too bad, but was he viewing his incarceration with rose-colored glasses because he was just so happy to be home that nothing else seemed to matter. He was rearrested not too long after his release, however, and was a terrifyingly emotional wreck at the thought of having to return to prison. I couldn't begin to imagine, with certainty, what my future would begin to look like starting next week.

Tuesday arrived and my bed number was shouted over the monitor.

"Roll-up!"

That's all I heard. I had everything packed awaiting this day. I took a quick shower and grabbed my paperwork off my empty bunk as YG had already taken my mattress outside for me. I gave him my commissary that I had left along with some extra clothing. Everyone said their good-byes. After I walked through the doors, I heard YG banging on the window. I turned around for a quick second as the officer cuffed me. He created a heart with his fingers and held it up. I pulled my hand up as the officer finished and clenched my fist, as if to declare that I will become the victor.

"Let me know where they send you, big bro," he shouted under the door crease.

He had to sound like a gangster after his little heart hand signal that was now clenched in a tight fist.

"Be good, my big bro," I shouted, stroking his ego. "Let me know when you get out and stay out of trouble," I held my fist up one more time as the officer instructed me to walk away.

Fighting Just to Dream

ALHAMBRA

The time I had spent at Durango was now over and my new journey had begun. The first stop was a holding tank at Lower Buckeye Jail where I remained for 24 hours. I alternated between the cold concrete benches and floors, and was given three Lamo bags to eat throughout the day. We were watched and monitored by an officer every 15 minutes. We made the best use of our time the best way we could, but the day was almost never-ending. It dragged on slow as a snail. We played cards and shared our experiences from our separate pods and jail. It was almost like a competition with each other to tell the craziest story. There were inmates that were headed to prison for days. Then there was Africa who was going to prison for 14 years. He had the longest time out of all of us in the tank. He had killed someone in a car accident driving under the influence. Everyone had different charges ranging from organized retail theft, drug possession, to manslaughter.

At six o'clock in the morning, we were told to line up and strip down. We were searched for the third time in 24 hours. "Strip naked, stick your tongue out, run your fingers through your hair, grab your balls and pull them up, turn around, squat and cough." At the conclusion of the search, we were given our old clothes and we all boarded a bus, destination Alhambra.

We got to Alhambra in minutes. The bus parked at the gate and waited for it to open. An officer came out and checked the entire undercarriage and went back to his post. We sat in the bus waiting to enter the prison. It took longer for them to let us in than to get here.

Finally, the big gate began to slide to the right. Exiting the bus, we were placed into holding tanks. We clutched our belongings under our armpits while we waited. There was a table in the middle of the courtyard with big manila envelopes. Each envelope had our last names and inmate numbers written on them. An officer came out of a side door followed by other officers. They began letting us out in groups. We had to place all our paperwork in their manila envelopes. We were lined up six at a time and we were taken to the side of the courtyard.

At this point, we were forced to squat down, as a K9 dog smelled our bodies for any contraband. The dog went down the line at least five times before we were taken inside a trailer. Here, we had to strip down naked, grab our nuts, squat again, cough and turn around to show the bottoms of our feet. We were all given a pair of underwear, a shirt, and a jumpsuit to put on. Everything was orange except for the boxers and socks. Anyone with tattoos was very closely examined for any hint of gang affiliations. I was questioned repeatedly about the number four that I had tattooed on my right arm. I informed them that it meant nothing in terms of gang affiliation, but instead it was my girlfriend's favorite number and also happened to be her initial. The officer scrutinized the number Four regardless and called over his senior officer. He had nothing to say but waved me on. We were taken into a room and asked information that pertained to our religion and health histories. X-rays were taken of our jaws and further dental history. We were required to take a picture, but first, we had to shave our beards.

I had been growing my beard and was frustrated by this dumb rule. I had to shave my beard for a picture but could grow it back right after. What was the purpose then? Only it proved our continued emasculation. I was required to sign documentation that instructed which family members of mine to contact in the case of my death while I was in state custody; a sobering experience to say the least. We were fed lunch and then it was right back to the rigorous schedule called intake.

We went through urine tests, conducted physical exams, and finally were evaluated by a team of psych doctors. Were we crazy? Hell, yes! We should be by now. No bed, no sleep for the past two days and left to lay on the concrete floors in the hallway. It got so bad that an older inmate started having seizures. Luckily, that was the wakeup call they needed to process us with some form of urgency. We were broken up into separate blocks. Each block was split into two runs.

These runs were called Dog Run or D Block, and Easy Run or E Block. D block was the last building on the yard. It was constructed like in an L shape. The tile floors always glistened from the constant free labor of inmates that cleaned it several times a day. The bigger cells were on the left walking into the building and segregation on the right. The hallways were well-lit as every three steps you were standing under lightbulbs welded over with steel to protect them from being broken by inmates. The only thing that separated D Run from E Run was a steel door.

It didn't matter what block you went into. Every single prisoner was locked down for 23 hours per day. We were only let out for a shower once every three days and on the weekend. We were crammed into these rooms like sardines. Convicts had to sleep on the floor because the cells were severely overcrowded. There were those inmates that had either committed dangerous crimes or had contributed severely to recidivism that would be taken out of their cells without warning and placed into segregation. They were deemed "too dangerous" and were not allowed to be around other inmates. The system was so inconsistent that one second a person would be taken to segregation for his level of security was said to be high, then by the next day he was back. They had made a mistake.

The first day that I was on the yard, I was walking to evening chow. This was the only hot meal of the day that we were given. During my walk, I spent my time admiring how beautifully cut the grass was. It was a vibrant shade of green, almost as if it had been painted with a paintbrush. The inmates that had come to call Alhambra home, walked around going about their business as usual but officers were scattered everywhere. They watched you enter and exit every single door. They watched as you walked from one side of the yard to the next. They watched as you carried out a conversation with a fellow inmate. There were CO's who were standing amongst the inmates throughout the yard as well. CO's were strategically positioned on top of the roofs carrying high caliber sniper rifles in hand. Jail had been like high school. This was a College!

Even though cameras or someone of authority monitored our every step, inmates still had their own ways of communicating. They spoke by using sign language or by speaking through the vents. Some even went so far as to fish messages and contraband from cell to cell. Inmates broke the bars that protected the lights then used lead from the pencils we were given to write with and twisted it around tissue to spark a fire to light their drugs or tobacco.

A lit coil-wrapped tissue paper was sent from cell to cell so that other inmates could light up their cigarettes and drugs that were in segregation. A lit tissue wrapper didn't come free but required a payment to the one at the source. He would receive tobacco and drugs for his service. The bathroom was the stash house and everyone got high in there. If a tile was loose then it had something hidden inside it.

I had become cool with Simpson. He was an Arizonian that enjoyed smoking cigarettes mixed with Spice. I would be his look-out once in the bathroom. I didn't smoke so I didn't mind and the duo worked well. He was aghast that I didn't smoke after he found out that I was arrested for marijuana. He was a professional marijuana grower himself and had stocks in a legal grow corporation run by himself and his childhood friends.

Simpson had gotten his startup money from growing and selling marijuana illegally in addition to robbing various other drug dealers. He was not the typical criminal. He was an educated family man who had been married since he was eighteen. He would even attend church on Sundays with his Mom. He was sentenced to two and a half years for drug possession after robbing a childhood friend. It wasn't the first time he had robbed him either, but this time he was fooled by the drugs he had stolen from his victim. He robbed $8,000 cash, five pounds of meth and over 1,000 pills he believed to be Xanax. These pills actually turned out to be a date-rape drug. He robbed his friend, then realized his phone had died from waiting on his victim for hours. He decided to walk home as he needed his phone to call his ride to pick him up. During his walk, he decided to take what he believed to be a Xanax. He took three of the pills because he thought maybe the Xanax bars were of low doses. The next thing he remembered was falling to the ground, unable to move.

He tried crawling but simply moving in general proved futile. He was slurring his words and his sentences wasn't making sense. He was in a residential area so he started to attract the attention of residents who were trying to help him. The residents called the police and ultimately, he was arrested. He woke up in jail days later. He was told that he had been uncontrollably vomiting. He was only charged for possession of meth. Both the date rape drug and the $8,000 were taken by the police officer who arrested him. The irony: he robbed someone and then was robbed himself.

"Errol, I'm done. Let's go before everybody start wondering where we're at," Simpson's voice was almost at a whisper as he hid the rest of his stash underneath a lifted tile he had discovered in the floor. "Never talk about something you won't do because life can all change in an instant," he said, almost as if he was telling himself that point rather than me.

I wasn't about to ask him what the hell he was talking about because the CO in The Bubble started staring right at us as she walked by. She ended the stare with a smile and said, "It's you two again?!" She shook her head as she stopped and followed us to our cell.

Simpson was high as kite and he would talk about the most random things. His train of thought would be derailed from one topic to another in seconds.

"Hey, do you guys want tohelp me out later?" the female officer asked.

"Sure," we both replied.

We jumped at the opportunity to help her out simply for the mere fact that we wouldn't have to be locked down. Simpson stared at her beautifully sculpted body as she opened the door and let us in. She hesitated as we got settled, peering into the cell. The second that she walked away, Simpson flew into a rampage of assumptions.

"Rude Boy!," he started yelling in chuckled laughter.

When anyone was excited as he was, everyone wanted to know why. Usually, that person had drugs or just found where he could barter for some. He swung his towel around his shoulder, holding it with both hands as he spun sideways and rocked back and forth. He continued turning to his audience.

"The sexy female CO likes Rude Boy. She kept looking at him when we walked into the bathroom. She checked him out when we walked back, and she sparked up a conversation so that she could talk to you. Bro! I'm telling you she likes you. We're going to see when she comes back to get us," he ended.

"Nah, brother. You're over-thinking things," I replied, trying to prove him wrong.

He would not be deterred as he carried on his quest to prove his point.

"She's been peeping you. She smiles at you all the time, brother," he elaborated.

"Yes, that's because I'm more of a social person than you are," I replied. "She's probably scared because of your crazy bald-headed look," I said.

We laughed.

I know that would have everyone cracking up. I always made fun of his bald spot in the cell and everyone would laugh at him. If anyone tried to talk to him that way, he'd have their head. With me though, he would just laugh and shake his head.

Sometimes, if I pissed him off like today, he would say I'm lucky that I'm big.

My tactics had worked. Everyone soon forgot the topic of our discussion and wanted to get in on the cigarette and Spice. Simpson and I became tight simply because we were bunkmates. We went to chow together and worked out together. We would gamble once in a while using cards that were made out of the box of milk cartons. He was twenty-two years old and had an extensive understanding of how to grow, clone, and harvest marijuana. He ran as a Kinfolk, but was half-Mexican. He spoke little Spanish but understood Spanish if it was spoken. Through our conversations, I realized he was very strong mentally. Although his past was not all that glamorous, he was highly ambitious and had plans of living right upon his release. Simpson had a small daughter that was his driving force for making right choices.

The only conversation that had been carrying on over the past ten minutes was Simpson's own. He went full circle into the same topic. He was adamant that the female CO had a thing for me. Even though these were the only words that I had been hearing, I could not seem to get the words that he spoke in the hallway out of my head.

"Never talk about something you won't do because life can all change that in an instant. What did you mean when you said that, Simpson?" I asked.

He smiled so wide that I could count every tooth in his mouth. "Rude Boy, all this talk about the sexy CO and you brought up what I said to you in the bathroom? You're crazy," he ended. "Are you going to tell me or not?" I snapped.

"I'm just saying that you tell me you're done with the game and all that but the way your eyes light up when I tell you about buds I've created I can tell that you are in love with the game. I'm just saying, don't ever say you won't do something because you never know. I'm not saying you have to do it illegally but don't knock it just yet," he ended.

I was confused because he himself said he was done living on the wrong side of the law too.

"He's right, Rude Boy," Sanchez joined in.

Sanchez was a Mexican who was born in America and classified as a Chicano. He had done two and a half years and was back on a parole violation to kill his number. Killing your number meant you'd rather go back to prison and finish your sentence rather than being free and being on a longer term of parole. He only had twenty-six days left before he completed his time. He was on a top bunk in our cell just as I was. We engaged in conversation from time to time. All he ever talked about was moving mass quantity of drugs and guns, so I listened.

"That's all you ever talk about. You're not done with the game," he stated. "A matter of fact," he paused, staring at me as if to wait for my reply.

He wouldn't get one. I was past tired of the game; I was exhausted. Sanchez just liked me for the fact I was a Jamaican and I was stand up when it came to the situations around. He was quiet most days but he listened to every word I had spoken. That was his basis for liking me. He wanted to do business with me on the streets. I'd tell him the same thing then, NO.

"I don'twant to go back to that life. I don't want to end up back here. It's as simple as that," I said.

I hadn't even served my time and everyone was trying to get me to do more. Sanchez was short and stocky. His chest was the canvas of a large tattoo of skulls, meaning see no evil, hear no evil and speak no evil. He was only twenty-two years old but already had quite an extensive drug-dealing resume. He was from a deep history of drug smuggling. His whole family was involved in the game, so he followed suit and was prepared to dedicate his life to it.

The conversation was quickly sidetracked with a typical escalation. It was frequent that we would have situations. It was inevitable when sixteen men were living in a 16x16 cell. Not to mention limited beds was a source for egos to implode when mixed with testosterone. Simpson called out Jersey who was a Wood. Jersey talked his way into and out of an asswhipping. He was good at talking and Simpson had enough of his mouth. Jersey would enter conversations that didn't concern him and he was a know-it-all besides. Simpson stood up and called him out for a second time, but Jersey refused to get up off his bunk. Simpson called him a bitch as he walked back to his bed to lay down. Sanchez and I looked at each other and laughed.

"I wonder how long Jersey's going to last in prison before somebody pushes (fights him regardless if he's fighting back). He talks too much and needs to mind his business," Sanchez suggested.

It wasn't long before the entire cell went quiet and everyone fell asleep. I laid on my bunk with my sheet covering my face to block out the lights that were shining above me.

Occasionally, a porter would pass and I would knock on the window asking them to flip the light switch off. Each time without fail though, a CO doing his fifteen-minute walk would notice the light was off and switch it right back on. While everyone slept, the room stood still. Egos had evaporated into thin air and tensions were deceased. The only noises were the occasional muffled snore or the buzzing of the cars passing on the road beside the prison. You could actually see the cars through a small hole in the wall as they passed. I began daydreaming but was quickly interrupted by the footsteps that I believed to be another passing porter. I rolled over to my side, only to see the female CO standing at the door of the cell. She began opening the door. She had come to collect Simpson and I to do some work. She had promised to let us out to roam the halls. This is our little get away and it came with jealousy from all the other inmates. To them we were being treated special. To me, I just wanted to stretch my legs mixed with the occasional conversation form a few inmates and the female CO. The rattle of her keys caused Sanchez to quickly sit up on his bunk. Face all scrunched up and rubbing his noise violently. He jumped up and put on his onesie.

"What are you doing?" I asked.

"Simpson's sleeping. I'm going for him since he's knocked out," he replied.

The female CO peeked her head in the door at me and smiled. She didn't care who came with her as long I was there it seemed. Her eyes twinkled like she was a little girl.

"I'm ready. Give me just a second," I said to her.

She watched as I put my shirt on followed by my pumpkin-colored onesie. I dragged my feet into my slippers and complained to her as I pulled my onesie up and latched it.

"This thing is too small for me. It's giving me a wedgie," I informed her.

She smiled then replied, "I'll see what we have in there. What size is that one you're wearing?" I started to pick up on what Simpson saw. I didn't respond with any sexual energy but more out of necessity.

"It's a 3x. I think I need a 4x, at least."

Before I could finish my thought, Sanchez tapped me on the shoulder. He pointed for me to walk out into the hall before waking any of inmates up. Jersey, naturally inquisitive, peeked through his sheet as we exited the cell and squinted at me as the CO closed the door. I was glad Sanchez was here.

"What's up with that weirdo Jersey. That dude just winked at me like he thinks something is up," I said to Sanchez.

"What! Rude Boy, I don't like him one bit, but if I smash him, I bet he would snitch," Sanchez stated.

"What are we going to help with?" he asked in his next breath. "I don't know, bro. I'm just glad to get out that cell," I replied.

I noticed that the officer didn't ask me where Simpson was. She didn't even care about our conversation. She just smiled.

"Move these mattresses from here to the corner for me, please. Reid, you could do those over there," she pointed to the matts next to her desk. "I'll give you guys some extra hot food trays," she ended.

We walked down the hallway behind her, flipping all the light switches off as we walked along. We made some inmates happy. At least for the next 15 minutes.

The hallway was in the shape of an L. Her desk was in the middle where she had a view both left and right. While in the hallway, inmates were passing messages to me to bring to other cells. I felt like a real porter for a second. On the higher yards, porters had the best jobs as they were out of their cells more than everyone else. For a moment, I envisioned that this must have been how it felt like. I had no more than ten matts to move and it took me well over an hour to do so. The officer looked up as I pretended I wasn't talking with other inmates and laughed. Sanchez was working hard. He wanted his extra tray. He came over and helped with my few matts left to be moved. The officer came and inspected our job then went on her routine walk. I was checking on a brother in solitary confinement that I had met my first day. He was signing to me, but I had no clue what he was saying. I just gave him a dap by pressing my hand on the glass and tapped on the door when the officer was in plain view.

We washed our hands in the bathroom and returned to the hallway to find the officer sitting at her desk. In front of her were two covered trays and chairs on the opposite side of her desk. Sanchez smiled and rubbed his hands together.

"Finally, time to kill this food! Rude Boy, please don't go telling nobody that we ate food now. All we did was move some mattresses," he warned, sitting down in the chair closest to the CO.

"You know that Simpson's going to know that we got food," I responded. "I can't lie to him about that. I could tell him that he snoozed so he lost but he's going to be mad that I didn't wake him up."

We both laughed and dug in while the inmates in solitary banged their doors in disgust of our royal treatment.

The CO left to do her walk again and returned about five minutes after.

"Do you guys need some wine with your meal," she said jokingly.

"Hell, yea," Sanchez joked along. Only he was really serious.

He was about his tequila but wine would suffice. "I'll take whatever you have!" he continued as we both laughed.

He looked at her in a sexual way. She looked at me as if I was to say something.

She sat down in the chair across from the table and observed us. She tapped the table with her pen and showed off her well-manicured nails. She had a beautiful fragrance that permeated the air and reminded you of freedom.

"You're welcome for the food," she said looking at Sanchez.

She began to question me.

"Where are you from? How long are you going to be here?" When I explained my story, it only sparked more interest.

She began to explain that I was too smart and handsome to be here. 'Here we go', I thought.

"I really don't know how you guys do it being locked up in that room all day. I know some people work here only to make your days living hell. I know you guys broke the law, but my job is to make sure you guys are behaving and not hurt each other. Not to provoke you daily."

She was coming from a stand point that I had never heard an officer speak on before. It was quite surprising.

"You're lucky I gave you extras. Everybody in this run is going to be mad I didn't give it to them," she changed the topic.

I got it she couldn't be too compassionate because of her job. Some inmates would take that as weakness, but I saw it as her strength. Even if she liked me, I was going to respect her for that comment. Everyone inside their cell watched from their windows. We were given the VIP treatment and they were all jealous wishing they had been the ones to get an extra tray. I wiped my mouth with the napkin and thanked her for the food. "No problem," she stated. "Thank you for moving the mattresses for me. They have been bothering me since they have been laying there right next to me," she continued as we stood up.

She walked us back to our cell and let us in, but not without exchanging some words with an angry Simpson.

Sanchez and I stuck to our story that we had not been given extra food but Simpson was one step ahead us.

"Rude Boy, I can't believe you're lying to me. I saw you guys from this window. Come look."

He grabbed Sanchez to the window to see his reasoning.

"Rude Boy! They saw everything," Sanchez said in a comic voice and hanging his head.

He was right. They saw half the table so they were looking at Sanchez the whole time. Everyone inside the cell was upset that we were the only ones given an extra tray, but that wasn't our fault. We were given a chance and we took it just as they would. We chatted all afternoon about our unique stories of life in the streets. For some reason I felt I wasn't a street dealer. I was more of a business man caught in the wrong business.

Sanchez' celly got up to pee. He had been in an accident previously and had lost one of his testicles. Now, he peed through a catheter. His story is one that proves that the very thing some of us wish for can be our greatest downfall. He received a lot of money from his insurance claim because of his accident. He started using drugs because of the pain he was feeling and ultimately had been arrested several times for possession. He destroyed his heart from drug use and now was simply being kept alive by a pacemaker. He rarely left his bed and didn't seem to have much life left in him. He was given tablets to take daily and was visited by the nurse more than anyone else in the whole block combined.

Every day, somebody would be rolled up and sent to prison. They went wherever had an open bed space for them. I had seen the psych doctor, taken the mandate, and had my physical done. Every day anxiety would set in around 2:30pm as new roll-ups would be called outside of their cells. Today, I had a feeling that I would be out of here. I started saying my goodbyes as the officer walked down the hallway, holding the list of new roll-ups in his hand. I got up and got dressed, walking around, confidently assured I would be leaving to a new prison. Sure enough, the officer stopped in front of our cell and began calling names. He called my name along with another Wood. We both rolled up and brought our cups with us. In Alhambra, your cup was your prized utensil. It meant you were able to get juice from the cafeteria. We lined up outside in the hallway and then walked across the yard, waiting for our names to be called once again. While in line, everyone else's name was called except for mine. I had a hold and had to return to the 24-hour lock down cell. Simpson and Sanchez had quite a blast, laughing at me because I had to stay. My hold was for medical and I had to wait three extra days before leaving. Medical had forgotten to do a TB Test on me.

Simpson ended up leaving the very next day. Sanchez wasn't going anywhere soon. He only had twenty-six days to do on a parole violation, thus he wasn't a priority. He complained every day that everyone was coming and going, yet he was stuck at Alhambra. He violated for having a dirty urine sample. He had been smoking Percocet and had never experienced a dirty test before. Since being here though, he realized that he was going through withdrawals. He would be so angry one minute but then the next he was so thankful for being here so that he could have a chance to kick his habit. He realized that he had grown dependent on the prescription pills. His only other worry was his best friend.

This guy had robbed another friend of two kilos of heroin and now he had a bounty on his head. In Arizona and the game, period, after an act like that, it was not uncommon for someone to turn up missing; even worse would to be found headless on the side of the road.

I quickly found myself becoming less talkative and more withdrawn since my first failed run of attempting to move on to a classified prison. The only person that I spoke to was Sanchez. He was still in his depressive state so I would encourage him to see the bright side of the situation. He was going through the pain today, but tomorrow was limitless if he made the right choices.

"Got to push through the pain to get to the gains my brother," I encouraged him.

We even started a workout routine right before lunch. We timed it that way so we wouldn't be starving. Well, the officers had different plans. They would feed us later than normal and we would be starving to the point that we drank water to fill us up.

The nurse had re-visited and informed me that I was finally clear of the TB tests and I was good to be transferred. Come to find out they had done two TB test on me; they had forgotten to call me back in time to check it. 'How unfortunate' one would think, but I was so positive, I shook it off. I was still here for a reason, that's what I told myself. Sanchez was doing good and working out was helping him to be less of a zombie. By simply motivating Sanchez to workout started to give me a good feeling about myself.

Four days had passed since my initial attempt to be transferred to a prison. Going to prison wasn't a bad idea compared to how Alhambra was run. Inmates spoke about walking the yard but most were most excited about the ability to smoke cigarettes. They spoke about basketball courts and softball fields. Prison began to look pretty cool to me. If there was one thing I had learnt from Sanchez it was that, "Not what we perceive to be help is always that. Sometimes help can become our pain and pain can become our help."

"Reid, roll-up," the female officer shouted.

She was the same officer that had a crush on me. I don't know why I didn't like her because she was very beautiful and carried herself well.

"Roll up," she said in a lower tone trying to imitate my Jamaican accent.

I smiled and gave her an A for effort.

"Told you bro," I said to Sanchez. "I knew I was leaving today." I walked with urgency and excitement in my step. While gathering my bedding and matts, Sanchez jumped down and pushed me back.

"Bro. Don't you know you're not suppose to do that. I'll do it," he commanded.

I wasn't going to complain. I was surprised that he would even do that. On a prison yard, Sanchez and I couldn't work out together, eat together, nor could he even speak to me depending on his Head. Suddenly, I was anxious to leave. I had gotten used to twenty-three-hour lockdown. Perhaps, even more so than that, I had fashioned my own way to survive Alhambra.

Big Jessie was an inmate inside our cell. He took my mattress and blankets because his were worn out. Sanchez, of course, took my extra blanket. The officer was so cool that she didn't even check my bedding when clearly all I took out was my matt and sheets. I was moving on from this tiny cell that housed sixteen people. Sanchez wasn't the sentimental type at all, but we shook hands before he exited the cell.

"Jamaica. You're one cool brother. It was nice to meet you. You'll be fine in the Pinta, homes. Time flies so fast. You'll be home before you know it. Remember," he paused and pointed at me with his index finger, "hollaat me when you get out."

I carried on. My second attempt to leave Alhambra in five days. Was this a foresight of my prison stint? Hopefully, I would finally be on my way without restrictions or cancellations.

All of the roll-ups lined the hallway listening for their names to be called. Once we heard our names, we had to repeat the last two digits of our DOC number to the Officer. The female CO called my name and smiled as I recited my final two digits to her.

"Reid, I need you to help me later to move some matts. I've got no help, but I have two extra trays today," she ended with a smirk that matched the sarcasm in her voice.

I returned the smile but no verbal answer. I was leaving. All the special trays couldn't convince me to stay here. We walked in a single-file line out of the building passing through several doors. Exiting the building, we walked across the basketball court, through two metal detectors, and then locked inside cages while we waited for our names to be called.

After about an hour had passed, a CO came and called our names from a piece of paper. He brought us inside and lined us up. We faced each other while following specific instructions that the Supervising Officer barked. Toeing the yellow line in front of us was our first order. The Supervising CO was backed by three members of his team that all stood scrutinizing each inmate as they walked by. They grilled you like a scene out of *Scared Straight*. Only, the next scene wouldn't be aired.

"Drop your bags! Put your slippers on behind you! Take your clothes off! I mean everything off. Hold it in front of you! Nobody put your clothes down until you are told to do so and when I say so, place them down behind you!"

While he was barking orders, the other COs were going by searching through our clothes, one piece at a time. They made us stick our tongues out and run our fingers through our hair. Everyone stood impatiently waiting to get this process over with quickly. Only, we weren't that lucky.

"Grab your nuts, your own nuts!" the CO clarified. "Pull them up! Drop them down! Turn around! Bend your knees and squat! Ok, put your clothes back on!"

Fighting Just to Dream

The CO's spoke amongst themselves as they tore through a large bin filled with clothes. Convicts scurried to put their clothes back on; boxers and socks only. The jumpsuits were taken and placed inside a big blue bin. Another blue bin was brought in by a separate CO containing orange pants and shirts. "Pick a pair of pants and shirt and put them on, then line back up! Nobody take more than one pair or you won't be getting any!" the CO shouted.

The power of his commanding voice made up for his short and stocky frame. He laughed as the inmates once dressed began to tease him about his size. They continued to instruct him to speak with his chest. Instead, it seemed his words were bellowing from his bulging belly that was creeping out of the bottom of his shirt.

"Line up in the hallway!" he yelled, walking as a seasoned body builder.

He pulled in his stomach, squeezing his chest with his arms up to the side and froze as he posed. Everyone laughed, even his fellow CO's that usually never cracked a smile. He walked over to the door and then flagged his hand for us to follow along behind.

"Stay here. Let me make sure the bus is ready for you guys," he explained, exiting the door after boldly flashing his badge to the camera.

"Excuse me," a female CO pleaded.

She was at the back of the hallway trying to squeeze her way down the middle of the two properly formed lines of orange. She squeezed her way through the inmates and her CO badge jerked as she bumped into a convict.

"Sorry, sorry," she repeated. "Coming through!"

She pressed the buzzer at the door and showed her badge and then waited. Just as she was about to step outside, she stopped and spoke into the monitor.

"Wait a minute. There are new inmates coming in and getting stripped down. It will only take 5-10 minutes at the most," she said as she stepped outside.

The door closed behind her. The door was tinted so that no one could see outside, but the hum of the engines outside seeped under the cracks. The short CO came walking back inside and began calling other convicts that had been waiting in the cages. He ordered them to walk through the middle of our two lines. They were the first to be escorted outside and then our group followed.

Paris was an older guy that stayed inside our cell. He furiously tried over and over to button his pants. He cursed at his pants as if they were his enemy.

"Fuck you, you stupid shit!" he yelled loud enough for all of us in line to hear.

Everyone laughed at him and he struggled on to fix his pants. As we walked outside, we listened for our respective names and then boarded our buses. Paris and I went on the same bus, as we were both going to the Yuma Correctional Facility. Paris sat next to me and was very excited. He was going to be passing through his hometown on the ride to Yuma. I sat in the back of the bus occupying a window seat.

"Gila Bend. Damn!" he exclaimed. "Man, Jamaica, I'm happy that I will be closer to home, but I'm going to be mad just driving through it! I'm glad we're going to the same yard though," he said looking out the window into the well-lit courtyard filled with inmates and officers.

He stared off further than he could see because he was silent until the bus was ready to leave.

"You're a real cool dude," he continued.

The bus driver stood up and counted everyone on the bus.

"We will be stopping at Douglas and that's where some of you will be making your final destination. Yuma guys, your next ride will pick you up from Douglas. I'm not a DJ so no complaining about the music either," he ended as he sat down in the driver's seat and began the journey.

Somehow, the thought of going to prison wasn't overwhelming as I suspected it would. I was getting this major hurdle out of the way so that I could create my new beginning. The beginning was soon to attract the end. That would signal my freedom and that was all that I could focus on. Besides, almost anything was better than being locked down in a cell 23-hours a day like I was at Alhambra.

We drove out of Alhambra by way of the main street, Van Bruyen. Chatter echoed through the bus as inmates were passing their respective streets they had lived on, hustled on, or simply frequented. They were recognizing restaurants they had eaten at, clubs they had been to, and even the Circle K that they would fill up after a night out. They would brag about robbing the store for cigarettes and stealing a few beers.

"Enjoy the sight-seeing guys," the CO shouted, his voice booming loudly over the sound of the radio.

"Turn the radio up!" a convict shouted as he stood up, holding on to the seat.

The shackles trembled around his ankles and it was with great struggle that he attempted to scratch his nose. If anyone wasn't admiring the scenery, I sure was. My eyes were glued to the window, peering through the bars. I was excited to see life buzzing about in the world I once enjoyed. Cars whizzed by and lights lit up the night sky.

From the skyscrapers to the village houses on the hillside. It was amazing to see society in its peak of the night. Even the vision of browning shrubs didn't seem so unsightly at the moment. The Cactuses all had their hands up and Police lights flashed as they pulled a car over in the tunnel, forcing the bus to switch lanes. We drove for hours and all that I saw was either new or pure unknown. The flat land gave way to miles bellowing across the desert land. The city was left behind and houses or any buildings at all became less frequent. The only thing to look at were the cars passing by or the white lines in the road.

The bus began to slow down, then took a detour from the highways on dirt back roads and unto smaller highways. We zig-zagged through the countryside taking back roads that were so dark that even the white lines became invisible. When we pulled up to Douglas, the wait at the gate seemed longer than the one-hour drive to the complex. The gates finally opened allowing us to drive in. The officer went directly to a gas station on the complex and filled up then dropped off three convicts. Backing out, we parked next to the 'Stick-em' Stiner DOC complex and waited for our new ride to appear.

Fighting Just to Dream

YUMA – LA PAZ

The bus arrived while the CO's were outside smoking cigarettes. They exchanged courtesies and counted handcuffs and foot shackles. The CO's checked through our properties, repeatedly counting each item to make sure nothing was missing. We exited one bus to board another that would finally carry us to our final destination: La Paz Prison, Yuma Facility. I had never heard of this yard before. A matter of a fact I hadn't realized this side of the world existed until now. Most of the stories I heard had been about 'Stick-em Stiner, 'Murda' Morey or 'T-Town' Tucson Complex.

"I'm glad I'm not going there," I said, speaking my thoughts aloud. "Going where?" Paris questioned, as if I had said something to him. I laughed.

"Nowhere, Paris. I was thinking to myself but spoke my thoughts out loud. I'm glad I wasn't going to Stiner or Morey. Hopefully, it won't be so bad where we are going."

"Yeah, I heard La Paz is a level two yard. There shouldn't be too much bullshit there," he spoke through his missing front teeth that created a lisp every time he spoke.

"Yuma, Tucson, Mogaby, Florence, Douglas, Kingman. It's all the same thing, brother. Any given day, it could legit be world war on any yard."

"I'm telling you. Only difference is some yards have more drugs and phones. That's it," he ended.

"Yeah, just what I wanted to hear," Paris stole the words from me. "How far is Gila Bend from here?" I inquired changing the subject. "It's about an hour. We'll be passing through Gila Bend soon."

He explained that when we left Douglas and hit the first stop sign, it was exactly thirteen miles from that point. He definitely knew these roads.

I continued to peek through the window, although the scenery was overtaken by darkness. Occasionally, a little light sparkled off in the distance. As we passed through Gila Bend, Paris anxiously pointed out all of the town's most historic and notable parts. He pointed his house out to me, but the excitement in his voice seemed to wane at that point. Sadness took over and the volume in his voice lowered until it began to crack.

"You'll be home sooner than you know it," I said as I instantly felt he needed some encouragement.

He agreed.

"Yeah, maybe two and a half years from now."

I placed my forehead directly on the window so that I could gaze directly into the lights. The cold glass felt therapeutic as I rested my forehead on it. I closed my eyes then reopened them hoping to get lost in all the lights that seemed so far away. I hoped that somewhere out there, everyone that I loved and cared about was doing okay. Maybe life after prison would be even better than life before coming here. I wondered if my girlfriend had calmed down since our last conversation. I needed her to be there for me, to reinforce the positive energy when I needed it. I had the tendency to get deep in my head and usually I told myself not the most inspiring things. I wanted to be there for her in every way that I could, even from such a distance. I really needed her strength right about now.

We drove for hours upon dirt roads, one-lane highways and back roads, primitive places, big cities and through the most beautiful hillside I had ever laid eyes on. The hills had roads winding through that led up to elevated plains that overlooked the borders of Arizona, California, and Mexico. The view was so majestic that one's thoughts became pure at heart. I saw the largest freight train that extended for miles, parked on its tracks. My son would have loved to see a train so long. The sightseeing journey that played out before my eyes allowed the actual journey of the drive to prison to lighten. Before I knew it, we had arrived at Yuma. It was surrounded by nothing but desert.

The Mexican border lights were in walking distance of the correction facility. After pulling in, we were made to exit into cages. After a few minutes, we were escorted out by three CO's and forced through the same rigorous search procedure of being stripped down to nothing. We were handed our ID cards and then entered through a set of gates, before being picked up by a minivan. The whole thing felt like a scene straight out of 'Orange is the new Black'. We were dropped off and each given a blanket, sheets and a horribly worn-out mat to sleep on. The CO stood by the main gate that led to our living quarters and radioed for the gate to be opened. We entered into my new home. I was going to be here for the next couple of months.

I had paid my rent in advance.

The light shone on us from the minivan that was still parked to our backs. The yard was fully lit, even in the darkness of night. It was three times the size of a football field and shaped like an oversized rectangle. The buildings were painted all white and had blue tops as roofs. Warehouses surrounded the workout pits and two basketball courts cradled the sides of a softball field. White sand lay all around decorated by long, orderly lines that were drawn by rakes. Barbed wire covered everything imaginable, with spikes lining every last surface that the eye could see.

"Damn, there are so many fences," I said, looking at the border lights through the wires.

"Those are here to keep you guys in," the CO said in a stern voice. "I was being sarcastic, Mr. Wise Guy," I replied as I walked away to my pod.

His eyes tried to burn a hole through my back the entire way.

It was 3:20am when I entered Building 6 F. I searched through the dimly lit room to find my bed number. 6F 41U. Night lights in the ceiling made everything appear to be blue.

The CO walked over and checked my ID. She requested that I be as quiet as possible while making my bed. I was given a top bunk. I asked the female CO if I could take a shower since I heard the water already running.

"That's no problem," she replied.

Through all of this, my cell mate lay still fast asleep. An inmate got out of the shower and dressed himself. 'This was crazy', I thought to myself in observance. 'Why the hell would he be getting dressed at four o'clock in the morning?' I realized my bunkmate was African American from his dark toned hand that hung over the side of the bed. I went to the bathroom and took a much-needed shower and followed that up with my prayers. I collapsed into my new bed, exhausted from a day full of travel, new adventure, and wonder.

"Hey," my new cell mate said followed by gentle taps on the side of my bed. "It's breakfast time. Are you going?" he asked. He put his glasses on as I replied.

"I'm still tired. Wake me up when you get back," I said.

I slept for a few more minutes but those minutes felt like hours. I was still exhausted from my travel all day yesterday. I was really exhausted from the thoughts that ran through my mind. I woke up as my cell mate had returned, tapping my bed.

"What time is it?" I asked him.

"About 7:30. They just called last call for chow," he muttered. "If you're going to eat you better go right now because they are about to close the chow halls."

My first impression of my cell mate was that he must be African, based on his tall stature and light accent. He was skinny and had very nappy hair that rolled up into balls or small as rice grains. "Thank you," I told him as I mustered the energy to get up and out of bed.

Walking outside, I noticed a sign on the door that boldly read: "ID and shirt tucked in before exiting the building." I ignored the sign, stopping to cuff my pants so that I wouldn't walk on them. I clipped my ID on and pushed the door open. The sun was already blazing and shone over every corner of the yard, making it impossible to find a bit of shade. Everyone was dressed in orange. They were buzzing about, carrying on their daily activities. I saw inmates working out, waiting in line for chow, playing basketball, and striking up card games.

I was new to the community and my first introduction was to a Muslim brother. He informed me that our table was at the back of the chow hall. Everyone had their own table. It was just like that in county jail, but in prison, they took things to a whole different level. Whites were called Whites not Woods. Kinfolks were called Brothers. Indians were called Chiefs and they had their own tables, unlike County Jail. They had a bigger population in prison so more privileges and power. They ran independently and had their own table on the yard. Whites had to pay taxes if they ran stores and anyone under the age of twenty-one couldn't do drugs or they would get smashed. Whites couldn't watch BET and were not to allow a Brother to sit on their bed. Pretty racist, if you asked me.

The Chicanos were broken down into smaller groups. The regular Chicano could do business and work out with a Brother if he so chose. The Cali boys, as the name suggests, were

Californian born. They weren't allowed to work out with or even to speak to the Brothers. The Brothers were also broken down into smaller groups of gangs. They had the West Side City Crips, South Side Crips and East Side Crips and Broadway Bloods or the Ave's. This only meant that you were from a certain area code. You were to rep your street and that was referred to as banging that area or your colors. There were also GD's, BD's and Black Mafias. The Pisas were still called as such, but they were broken down into Border Brothers and Cartels such as Sinaloa, Nogales and Michoacan. The Border Brothers meant that they ran the Mexico and United States Border. They held a high title amongst their people. They were heartless as they'd kidnap innocent civilians crossing the desert and use them as drug mules. Pisas and brothers remained a cliqued and Whites, Chicanos and Chiefs did the same.

I introduced myself to a Brother as Jamaica since that's what most people called me. He immediately replied, "There's three Jamaicans here. You're Jamaica #4".

"Aright. Jamaica #4 it is," I agreed, sticking to my plan of 'the fewer words, the better'. The chow hall was more spacious than county jail but nothing to talk about. The food a little better as I had pancakes with some type of meat that I couldn't make out.

I left from the chow hall and the sun's beam was unbearable. It was only eight o'clock in the morning, yet it was over a 100 degrees. I quickly realized that this was what it meant to be in the desert. The sunlight proved that the walls were not in fact white, but cream colored. It also proved that the blue painted roofs were being worn out.

I had a welcomed hot breakfast for a change. Walking on the yard, everyone could tell I was a new face around these parts. I was stopped a million times but kept it short and spicy. I wanted to sleep and that was my only intention. "Where are you coming from? How long you got?" the questions kept pouring in.

"Year and a half," I replied, "and I'm coming from Alhambra." Since everyone seemed to have the same questions, I attempted to answer them before they were asked.

I stopped outside of Building 6 as I recognized my cellmate was talking to his friend. I thanked him for allowing me to get some extra sleep. He knew how it felt to be brought on that long bus ride so it was nothing to him. He continued to speak with his friend and I found myself twisting and turning, scanning the yard. Paying attention to the fine details that I had missed last night. I was also studying my new neighbors that inhabited La Paz. There were monkey bars, push-up blocks, and ab stations spread out all over the yard but there was not a weight in sight.

"Have you met Jamaica over in Building 5? I think his name is Kevin," my cell mate asked.

"No, I don't think so," I replied.

I had just barely arrived and had spent a greater number of hours sleeping than awake. Plus, this hot sun wasn't motivating me to move and explore the environment in anyway.

"There he is right now," my cell mate stated pointing in the direction of a bunch of inmates coming around the bend of the tracks. It wasn't easy to differentiate amongst people when everyone had on an orange outfit.

I spun around to look in the direction that he pointed. Sure enough, I recognized the Jamaican. He was coming around the bend of the track and stood about 5'8" with a stocky build. He was as dark as Blue Mountain Peak coffee, fully bearded, and with a white streak mixed throughout. He wore a winter hat and had dread locks hanging from the back that were tied together by elastic bands. He hid his eyes behind a pair of dark, Dolce & Gabbana sunglass that seemed to match his skin tone. His fresh pair of New Balance sneakers matched the tracksuit he wore. "Yo, what up?" he inquired slowing down to a complete stop.

He immediately shook my hand. Knowing that he was Jamaican, I replied, "Wa gwan, Rude Boy?"

He leaned back, pausing for a couple of seconds.

"Yo, the man a Yardie?" he asked rhetorically.

"Yeah man, born and bred," I replied.

He seemed to forget he had been jogging just seconds before as we found ourselves suddenly deep in conversation. He quizzed me on where I was from in Jamaica and where I lived in the United States.

He assumed I was here for marijuana, as that fit the stereotype that is commonly assumed of Jamaicans. Sadly, he was right. "Where do you stay at?" he asked.

I was a bit confused, as I had already answered that question. He spun around as if to look at the buildings and then I realized that he meant what building was I staying in here.

"6 F41 Upper," I said, directing my view toward the building behind me.

Up close, I realized he didn't have dreads, but his hair was twisted and held together by elastic bands. He was full of energy and was excited to meet another Jamaican. Typically, Jamaicans were tall and skinny so the fact that I was big and bulky he thought I was a 'Jamerican': An American born of Jamaican parents.

"You need anything, Rude Boy?" he asked, taking off his sunglasses and fixing them neatly into the string of his sweatpants.

"Nothing yet, Rude Boy," I answered, giving him a dap to show my appreciation for the thought. "I've got money on my books. I should be good with the first commissary that I get. I just need my things from property though. Do you have any idea when I might be able to get them?" I asked him.

"No idea," he said as he shook his head. "Sometimes they give it to you right away and other times they can take a few weeks." We continued talking for a few minutes, switching from Patois and back to English all in the same sentence. My cell mate was intrigued by our accents and interrupted to ask a question. "Kevin, I've never heard you talk like that before. What is that?" Kevin laughed and then spoke.

"That's Patois. This is a real Jamaican so I can finally talk Patois again," he ended, still laughing.

We began walking and talking while we circled the track. Everyone passing by stared at us and would stop or go out of their way to say what's up to Kevin. He knew everyone and everyone definitely knew him. They all greeted me just for the mere fact that I was in his presence. After we had finished a few laps, we stopped at his house (his cell). He gave me some commissary since commissary was a week away. He decided that I needed some food to carry me through. We spoke and laughed as if we were two long-lost friends that had been reunited. He hadn't been to Jamaica since he had arrived in America and had so many questions for me. Just two years ago, I had been back to celebrate my birthday on the island so I had seen it more recently than he had. He certainly possessed the attitude of a true Jamaican. He portrayed himself as one by the way that he dressed, spoke and did business all at the same time loved by others or so it was portrayed.

Not even an hour later, Kevin had brought me a TV and told me whom I had to pay for it once I received my commissary. I even got a sweet deal. My cellmate was very surprised to find me watching TV once he came back inside. He laughed and shook his head, "only you Jamaicans". I think for a moment he might have thought that I was pulling a fast one and watching his tv, but that was until he turned and noticed his was right where he left it.

"Damn!" he exclaimed. "You have a tv already? Only you Jamaicans. That's crazy," he repeated.

He began helping me to fix the wires so they wouldn't be in the way. He programmed my tv so I'd get the info to pop up when it was turned on. My cellmate began to lecture me on the way the yard works and told me about his prison stints in Vegas. He had 'Black Mafia' tattooed across his stomach from joining the gang in prison. He was also Muslim and had his Quran wrapped up neatly in a scarf like material on the desk we shared, but asked me never to touch it.

In only two weeks, I had paid for my tv and was rocking some clean New Balances. New Balances were the best thing you could get, so of course I had to get them. Many couldn't afford them though. I was hanging out with Kevin more frequently and began to see a whole lot more of prison than I knew existed at first. Anything you wanted could be peddled in if you paid the right price. Kevin wanted me to delve right in, but I insisted on sitting back and seeing how the flow of yard was first. I think that might have impressed him more as I showed I didn't need him as well as I wanted to learn from others mistakes rather than my own. Inmates all numbered were buzzing about as if it were the market. Pumpkins ran the track, played dominoes, sold tickets to bet on basketball games, smoking, cooking big tubs of food. Oh, the food caught my attention. I immediately walked in their direction.

"What's this y'all making?" I asked.

"Burritos! Five-dollar Burritos!" the Mexican paused to grab a squeeze cheese to spread all over three tortillas.

"Yow! You don't want that. There is pork in it!" Kevin informed. "No worries. Later, I'll have them make some without pork for you and me," he ended, patting me on the shoulder. He was the man and I was the new comer but for some reason I felt he felt something unique about me.

The burrito sure looked good but there were pork rinds in it that I didn't eat. Later on, these same guys would deliver me an eight-dollar burrito that Kevin had purchased. I couldn't eat it all; I shared it with my cell mate and Big O. Big O, was a character I had met in my pod that always had me laughing. Everyone feared him but thought he was funny.

After a couple of weeks, I realized Kevin was never at his cell. He was either at the domino or poker table gambling. I didn't play poker so he had me watch and learn but I grew tired of watching poker and decided to learn to play chess. Watching him play poker taught me one thing, 'Play the opponent, not the cards!' I was hooked at chess even though everyone I played against beat me. They all taught me different moves though and I wanted to learn so bad. I played the worst and the best and they all taught me things. The pieces had no use until they were used with intent. I got so hooked, I played with myself even when no one was available. Kevin and I had started working out in the mornings and we began to break down the parts of the process that I didn't like. The probability was too great to have mistakes. I wanted to make money and lessen my chances of being exposed. There had to be a better way, and until I found that, I was sitting out. He understood and informed that he'd have a few run ins with the officers. He was currently under investigation and yesterday he had received a ticket for conspiracy to introduce contraband.

He was determined to fight this conspiracy to introduce prison contraband but the officers were growing tired of his disrespectful attitude. That's the only element he lacked. He couldn't understand that we were not invincible and that we needed to guard ourselves by blending in. He just couldn't kill his ego. That meant the less you had run ins with the officers, the less your name would be mentioned. Instead, his name was trending like Twitter feeds. In two weeks, Kevin had racked up two other minor tickets that made the warden bump his score up without even allowing him the right to appeal his case. He was given three months extra time and his scored increased so high he would be going to a higher yard. Neither the COs nor the Warden had any evidence of his misgivings, but his name was ringing too many bells. They were suspicious of one of his people that got caught that might have told but those were just allegations. No-one knew anything for certain.

Kevin spent the rest his days relaxing or gambling. He ran a few stores on the yard and had other inmates working for him. They collected tax, which is another way of saying that they were paid interest for loaning food equivalent to a fixed amount of dollars. To see Kevin go through all this process without a shred of evidence against him made me think. If I was ever going to take part in the prison game, I was going to be layered like an onion.

Either way, I wanted to be the regular inmate that just liked to stay to themselves but enjoyed the finer things, even in prison. I wanted no light shone on me and I wanted to remain anonymous to the officers if that was possible. If not, I wanted to be known for doing the good things such as playing sports or educating others.

After Kevin left, I rarely spoke to anyone. I observed how convicts operated and how the CO's paid attention to the finer detail, just as I was doing. Kevin had left some gambling debt behind and I promised him I would handle it. I paid the inmate he owed. That payment led to the information that he could get me anything I desired. I thought of the sun and how it was affecting my eyes. I requested a pair of ray bans. Later I purchased a pair of Ray Bans off him and quickly realized how different I was treated. I always had commissary and cooked every single night, but there was something about these Ray Bans that caused people to start paying close attention to me.

And that included the COs. Where I had been virtually unidentifiable amongst a sea of inmates, now I stood out. It didn't help my cause that I had gained over thirty pounds and was 270 pounds with a 6'4" frame.

Fighting Just to Dream

Being on a yard where some convicts were serving 25-year sentences and others just days, allowed me to gain great perspective. I noticed how the two interacted amongst themselves and others. The OG's, as they are called on the yard, dressed well every day, even though they had to maintain their status on and off the yard over the years. Their shirts were always tucked in and they walked with a swagger that displayed a certain level of confidence and respect. They had an air of entitlement about them and they lived up to it when they had conversation or were physically challenged. The Short Timers, or anyone serving less than five years, held the opposite mentality. They hated prison. They broke every rule they could get away with. Their pants were never above their waists, their clothes not cared for, and they tended to be loud and obnoxious.

I gravitated to the OGs since they showed more respect for one another. One OG really struck something inside of me and we quickly became friendly. One regular day way back when, he woke up to find his son had been murdered, his lifeless body lying on his front lawn. Rumors flew that the killers resided in the community. He was enraged and began a manhunt of his own. The authorities pleaded with him in hopes of persuading him to leave the matter at hand up to them, but he was destroyed by his son's murder. He felt disrespected by the manner in which they threw his body in the front of his yard for all to see. He wanted them dead and he wanted to do it himself. Before he could accomplish his goal, two of his other sons were killed together in a drive-by shooting. This pushed him to near insanity. His wife died suddenly after she had a heart attack but he would tell you she died from a broken heart. They had lost three sons in a four-month time period. He was forced to carry an overwhelmingly heavy load and the burden felt like he had the weight of the world on his shoulders. He had been a veteran who served in the military and was deployed to Vietnam. Killing a person didn't scare him. He had done just that as a part of his daily routine. He called it eradicating threats. He continued to search for his son's killers. He allegedly shot at one of the individuals the community was saying participated in his son's murder. He was arrested and while awaiting trial, he found out that the person he had shot at wasn't a suspect after all. He was overcome with relief, as he was thankful that his rage didn't end the life of an innocent man.

After losing three sons and his wife, he faced an attempted murder charge and he did so only days after burying the love of his life. He took the first plea and was given a reduced sentence due to his military past and the losses that he and his family had incurred. Through all of this, he was almost relieved that he was going to prison. Prison provided him space from the outside world that he needed so badly and it also gave him a chance to find himself once again. He had been incarcerated for over a year now and had more drive and motivation to succeed than ever before. He had been taking college courses and was close to completing his Associates degree. He was then following that up with a Bachelor's degree. He and I brainstormed daily and had a list of ideas in which he could generate income upon leaving prison.

He was excited to have met a college graduate that lived in the same building. He loved that I was able to help him with his studies and correct his writings. He was blown away by my entrepreneurial mindset, but at times he'd remind himself that all drug dealers were entrepreneurs. He couldn't understand why I hung out with Mr. Trouble: Big O. He was sure that Big O was going to bring some form of trouble, but I had plans for Big O that no one understood just yet. I saw a hole in the system and I was going to work it. First, I was going to help Big O and he would be indebted to me and would work with me in my plot. He was going to be the focal point, all whilst making money himself. He was getting into trouble and not making money, so I knew he would jump at the chance once money was involved. I wasn't one sided. Paucity was never my forte. I was always aware of the bi-phasic effects, so I dedicated time to the internal as well as the external. I was reading more than ever to cement my persona as a good ol' Boy.

Big O was my Gorilla. He had been my friend from day one. He was six-foot-one with skinny legs but a massive upper body. He was prison build. He wore his head shaven bald and hardly grew any facial hair. He rocked back and forth as he walked and his bulging twenty-two-inch arms were pronounced even when wearing a sized 6 XL shirt. As big as he was, he never scared me one bit. He was the man on the forefront but my puppet on a string. The system was set. Big O would make the orders and pick up the delivery. He would break it down and let me know the count. He would hold the commissary at his house and we would move them to my house at three in the morning. Kevin would have been proud of me. My plan was moving flawlessly. That was until Big O began to gamble and rack up bills and inmates started to take his debt out of his payment. He was furious he wasn't making the money but would be jealous of what I had. No matter what was going on, he was in good hands. I paid his debts and we continued to work with an understanding that this wasn't going to happen again. Then I found out an interesting fact. Big O said he didn't smoke Spice, but he did. I was furious and called him out on it. He was extremely mad because I told him I wasn't going to use him anymore to be my front. He brought me all the money he owed me over a couple days to persuade me to keep him on board.

Rethinking my decision wasn't a possibility and it happened that I had definitely made the right decision. I started limiting my contact with him and everyone saw it. They all made their comments and jokes about the situation. Big O was offended when his friend, Big Chris, the Head of the yard called him my slave. In similar fashion, Curtis West kept saying that he was running errands for someone that could be his son. Curtis was recently brought to the yard and was a west side city Crip. He kept poking insults at Big O. Big O kept advising that we work together with Curtis, but I was reluctant. I didn't know Curtis or the type of person he was. Curtis began playing the devil. He began telling Big O that I was working out to get big so that I would kill him. Everyone knew Big O was schizophrenic and that he was gullible. What began as a joke escalated quickly into something serious. While I was in the bathroom taking a shower, Big O came walking in, yelling my name.

"Rude Boy! Rude Boy!"

"What's up?'" I answered slightly pulling the curtains to peek.

"Brother, before you kill me or I kill you, let's just go our separate ways. All these dudes disrespecting me calling me your slave and what not. Matter of fact too…"

I stopped him before he could even finish.

"O! You know my only rule in the shower is what?" I asked.

"You don't want to talk to anyone while you're in the shower,'" he ended.

"Exactly! Talk to you when I get out. Right now, I'm taking a shower," I ended.

I got fired up when I saw him tuck his shank back into his waist. While I showered, I got angrier by the second. I was naked and this man thought it was cool to come in here on some bullshit. I got dressed and went outside to talk to him. I called him away from the crowd and began talking.

"Bro, what part of that shit you just did is cool? WHAT THE FUCK IN THE WORLD IS SERIOUS FOR YOU TO TALK ABOUT YOU KILLING ME OR I KILL YOU?" I paused for his response. "Bro, you brought a shank in the bathroom for what? You coming to talk? That in no way can be justified, brother."

Standing next to Big O, I felt like hitting him over his shiny bald head. This man had lost his memory. He forgot I was the one that stashed his shanks when they came to search his house. He must have forgot that I still looked out even when everyone said to leave him alone. Mentally, I had already prepared for a battle.

"Brother, I'm sorry. You do look out for me and you've taught me a lot. I learn so much from you, but you know I'm crazy. I love you, bro-bro," Big O ended.

I laughed sarcastically. How dare this man say he loves me when his motto was 'fuck family and friends'. He was so set on his path that he had both tattooed on his forearms. If that wasn't enough, he had to throw in the schizophrenia excuse. This was his 'pity me' trick, but I had heard enough.

"Whatever you got left for me, consider it a tip. Brother, I'm good. You don't mess with me and I won't mess with you, just like you said in there."

"I just wanted to say I'm sorry, Rude Boy," he started off by giving me a dap as soon as I walked under the Ramada where the phones lay.

His entire demeanor and body language threw me off completely. It wasn't what I expected to hear, nor did I expect him to be sitting down and looking at me with remorse in his eyes.

"I respect all that you do for me, bro and I love the positivity that you talk all the time. Sometimes, it's just that I be thinking that everybody is trying to get me. I wake up sometimes thinking that my neighbor, Johnny, is trying to kill me and that's why I walk around with that lock in my pocket. You have to understand, bro, I've done a lot of time. Some people are way more fucked up than me. I've been locked up for murder since I was eleven. I've spent more time in prison than I have spent on the street. Shit, I grew up in prison! This shit is all I know. My bad, bro, I'm sorry for talking all that crazy shit to you. You know I'd bust anybody's head that tried to mess with you," he smirked as he dapped me again.

I respected and appreciated what he said and I guess I understood where he was coming from. Still though, a serious agreement had to be made.

"That's all good but that's got nothing to do with what you said to me inside. Mr. Woods talks all that shit about me adopting you and you laugh, but Big Chris says one thing about you being my slave and you trip! I know they're just hating because he asks me for food every time himself, too. That shit you just pulled in there, just now, makes me not want to fuck with you and that's some real shit! I tell you to stop telling people the shit you be hustling is mine and you're constantly bringing people to me still. I don't do business that way. If you want to squash this then that's fine, but from now on, I'm going to do me and you do you. It's the best way, brother. I still fuck with you but from a distance," I ended.

"But," he stuttered, "but you...you don't know about...". "Homie, I know what I'm talking about. Just do your thing and pay me when it's time," I ended my rant.

"Alright, bro," he said reluctantly. "Man, just know that I've been through some real shit. I love you, bro," he said, as I dapped him and walked off.

"Stop telling me that shit, Homie. Respect is enough. I don't fuck with that love shit. Love your family. You barely know me. We're cool though. Don't sweat it," I said, holding the building door open for a White boy who was trailing behind.

We were definitely polar opposites. He looked at life from a totally different point of view. As much as I pretended that I didn't need him, I did. And I needed him to play that role perfectly. I was tall, muscular, and relatively quiet. I didn't speak too much but when I did, I got right to the point. I didn't tell pointless jokes and stand around and laugh with everyone. All that was pointless to me. My demeanor intimidated a lot of people, whether I meant that or not. Even though I was diplomatic and people usually felt comfortable enough to speak to me, I kept it formal and always spoke my mind freely, whether it was what they wanted to hear or not. Big O liked that about me and I liked that everyone was terrified of him. When I sent him to collect, they either had to pay their bill or go get their money from another store to pay me. If only he could stop bringing heat to me then everything would be fine. He ate when I ate and it could all be that simple. I would rather read my books and spend my time improving my financial literacy anyways than worrying about the Police.

It wasn't until a few days after our discussion that O brought me some money that he had collected.

"I told you that I got you, Rude Boy. All these people be talking but none of them got you like I do. You put me on and I would literally kill for you," he ended, getting so serious that the skin in his forehead cracked in the middle.

"No need for that, my G. We're getting our money. There's no need for all that extra shit. That only brings nothing but negativity," I replied, counting the money out in front of him to make sure that it was right.

There is nothing that I hated more than someone telling me that they gave me money and then finding out that it was wrong. If it was over, then "thank you, come again. I enjoy doing business with you and appreciate the tip!"

"Wasn't it just last week that you were mad as shit because they shut the yard down? The dude PC'd up with your money and now he's gone and you're left dry. Be diplomatic in a situation first, my G. You don't have to act like a gorilla all the time, especially if there is no need for it," I said to Big O.

"Shit, I ain't got it like you, so I can't be like you," O replied.

I laughed because this was always his defense. According to him,

I was blessed and highly favored because I had money on my books and a support system at home.

"Do you remember when I first got here?" I asked him in a dramatic fashion.

"Yeah," he replied.

"Aight, so what are you talking about? I came here wearing slippers on my feet and barely had commissary for the first week. Kevin hooked me up, but I had to wait for my sneakers from property. I couldn't make any phone calls. I had to buy three-way calls every single day. I wasn't shit then, right? I ain't shit now either. I'm just me. I make shit happen because of my attitude. If you want to perceive me in the way that you do, just like everybody else, then that's up to you. That boss shit you talk in front of everybody though, cut that shit out."

I could barely breathe trying to get my words out so fast. I was tired of the same shit, all of the time. The whole "I'll kill anyone for you," phrase was resonating through my head. Why would somebody even bring that up? Every day he was quoting bible verses, reading the bible aloud and then telling me how many people he killed. It's unbelievable. He still talked about banging people's heads in with the lock that was stuffed in his sock. I knew I had to reevaluate and break ties. I was going to have to fall back completely from O.

James and I started kicking it more and true to form, Big O would always threaten him. James would tell me what was said and laugh at how crazy Big O was. This was starting to get crazy. Big O wrote me two letters and I felt like they were coming from a girlfriend! His letters sounded like he was jealous that I was kicking it with James, aka Bam Bam, as everyone else called him. I let James read the letters to make sure that I wasn't the one going crazy. James would reiterate that I was only trying to help him make some bread and agreed that Big O's sensitivity definitely got the best of him on this go-around.

Fighting Just to Dream

Yardie, my Jamaican OG, came and told me to chill on my store since my partner had gotten rolled-up and the yard was hot. The Special Services Unit was conducting more searches than usual. I let James and Iraq know that I had fallen back and would just relax from now on. I was interrupted in the middle of my conversation when a White boy pulledup at my bunk and was talking crazy. He claimed that Big O had told him that I had something for him and that he needed a clip.

"I don't know what you're talking about, my G," I said, clearly dismissing him.

I ended the conversation entirely, fully understanding the importance of making sure that I went to clarify this situation with Big O. Before pursuing the issue and creating a bigger one, which surely he would have, I was able to come to my senses. I knew I didn't have anything, nor was I doing anything wrong so if they wanted to talk, let them talk, and if they wanted to search, let them search.

James decided he would start working out with Wayne and I. We switched our schedule up, moving our night workouts to five o'clock in the morning. The heat had come to the point of being unbearable, even by 9am. By nine o'clock in the morning, it was 105 degrees and it was 120 by 11 am.

Inmates continued to approach me, talking about Big O. He was telling inmates that I stopped messing with him and I left him in a bad place. The fact of the matter was, I never discussed anything with anyone; I had nothing to say. Big O's daughter's birthday had arrived and I ordered some post cards for him to send to his daughter. I was able to hook him up with some hygiene products that he needed, but right after I kept it pushing. I came here by myself and I owed nobody here anything. Whomever I chose to befriend was my choice. I became irritated by the persistent attempt to discuss the same petty drama. Prison was worse than a junior high school because it thrived off the gossip. The more seasoned convicts seemed to flourish in these combustible situations, presumably because they made the time pass. I planned on passing my time in a very different way though.

I had been ferociously reading since my arrival in Yuma and with all the events that continued to occur, reading was my sanctuary. What essentially began as a way to pass time, turned into a passion for learning, growing, escaping, and experiencing all that life had to offer. What I read always translated to far more than simply written words, as those words were the means by which I traveled my daily journey. I meditated on parts of my studies. At times, I'd write the complete pages into my dairy and re-read them sitting outside under the Ramada. When I read, I travelled far outside of those prison walls.

The first book I read was of a South African Kaffir (mulatto) family's experience. I continued to read more books and each book led to another. *Rich Dad, Poor Dad, Vybz Kartel: The Voice of the Ghetto, Passion Profit and Power, Second Chance; For Your Money, Your Life and Our World, There's a Sucker Born Every Second, Changeology* and *Rich Dad's Guide to Investing*. Upon completing a book, the elders and I would sit and discuss every aspect of it. We would brainstorm ways that we could implement into our daily routine, even whilst still in prison. We broke down the book's concepts and began writing these concepts into our post-release daily plans. This partnership became something that each of us valued. Our makeshift Book Club not only helped us to pass time, but it allowed us to reaffirm a purpose within ourselves. Every single day, our hunger for books grew exponentially. I, on the other hand, was taking on more and more responsibility dealing with a lot more individuals and a lot of their issues.

At this point in time, I had come to accept the fact that I was in prison and that I would not have the ability to simply wake up one morning and ask for this nightmare to be over. I knew I had to serve my time, regardless of how I felt about it. I was going to be released one day, so I built the concept that I better spend my time wisely and make the most use of it. I bought a Spanish to English language Rosetta Stone set from another inmate and I began to pursue a dream of mine. I wanted to learn Spanish. I nullified a popular prison saying that you hear often on the yard, "There are only two days that matter in prison: the day you go in and the day you get out." Instead, I promised myself again that from that day forward, I would learn something new that would better my life and my future. There were suckers born every day and I wasn't going to be one. It was simple, 'eat or starve'. I wanted to eat of all the knowledge I could find. The fact that most overlooked that you could eat forever and not just everytime you were starving. I hungered for my own but knew patience and consistency had a huge role to play. I wanted to build my own. I didn't know where to start but that was exactly what I needed to do. Starting would motivate me to learn more about the business to excel. I was always competitive and of course, I naturally want to be the best.

Furthermore, if a system could own my body for eighteen months, I was going to own my mind and a business soon for damn sure.

I had a definite purpose and stayed clear of meaningless gossip and even began to use every conversation that I held each day as a mode by which to perfect my communication and interpersonal skills. I thought of myself as a Boss. I was the owner of my first Business, Errol Reid, LLC. I wasn't going to build an empire if I first couldn't even build myself. My eyes were beginning to open but the temptation of the game was overwhelming. I had become a Young OG on the yard that everyone respected and so many people came with ideas that I already had myself. It was the opportunity I was looking for. Go through someone else and nothing could come back to me but food and money on my books. It made sense and so I started to break down the very people I was encouraging to build themselves.

After only a few short months, I started having a love-hate relationship with selling drugs. Becoming 'The Man' wasn't of interest to me anymore because Wayne and I were the Kings of La Paz. I was 'The Man' without the game, but it sure gave me validation to spend money and help others out because I could. I had made significant progress in my short time financially and mentally. Though I had daily failures that would frustrate me, I remained positive. I continued to push myself every day to be a better person than the one I had been. A matter of fact, it came to the point where I realized I wasn't a man for almost a year before prison. I wasn't fulfilling those responsibilities. When I fell, I would pick myself up again and get myself right back on track. It wasn't that easy after my initial arrest. Days after that, I just survived. When I was motivated, I would get into negative conversations that stole my energy. I gave up my power to meaningless arguments and influences and took losses both financially and mentally.

I didn't want to be here; nobody wants to be in prison, but it was rehab for me. Even with such a positive attitude, I missed my family and my friends and I grew tired of the same old routines. I still devoted my time to doing only those things that would better my life and the lives of those around me. My excuse for selling drugs was, ' I helping guys so why not'. The Bible justified it to as it refers to the point that, 'no one listens to wise man if he doesn't have the riches to prove his wisdom'. It was only for a little time anyways for I wasn't going to do this when I got closer to my release date. No way I was going to jeopardize getting any extra time.

Riches wasn't what I was striving for, but rather wealth; wealth in love and life. I yearned for a stable and happy relationship. I dreamed of being able to make memories with my kids and enjoy life. I wanted simplicity and honesty even while embracing day to day challenges and those that were sure to come with my release. It would be easy to feel sorry for myself and not take responsibility for my actions. That way, I could shift my responsibility onto others. Many people walked that road but those are not people that I will pass on my own journey. My road was going to be different. I was going to walk with doers and achievers. I simply refused to ever allow myself the option of taking the easy way out.

There was one person on the yard that seemed intriguing to me. He was only a few months older than I, but he acted differently. He was loud and boisterous. I admired something about him but we had never even spoken much as I tended to stay clear of those who liked to draw attention to themselves. He was in an Alcoholics Anonymous class, and from listening to the way he spoke, it seemed as if he really did want to better his life. I studied him over time and finally decided that I felt comfortable engaging in conversation with him, hoping that he was able to control his tongue. It wasn't too long after that we became friends. I admired his ability to remain positive, even though he had a lot of debt on the yard. He had the air of an intellectual, even though he had never graduated from high school. His life hadn't always gone as planned and he became a hustler. He was forced to step up and help his mother pay the bills at a young age. Being a young father himself, he felt an insurmountable amount of pressure and responsibility.

Even through all of the negatives that life kept throwing my new friend's way, he was resilient and did his best to always stay positive. One thing though; we ended up arguing about our relationships nearly every damn day! Doing time and having no worries was nothing. If you had no family, no support, no real purpose, then it might make sense to adapt to the mind-numbing routines and just survive. Never truly living. Never creating anything for yourself to call your own when released. Not even yourself. Maintaining a relationship with someone on the outside can be a big challenge. He argued with his girlfriend about things that he had done in the past, as did I. In the short fifteen-minute conversation that he was able to have with her, she would always somehow bring up the darkness of his past. It was funny because I listened to his stories and it was so easy for me to see where I had been wrong in my past. But arguing about the past, while in prison, didn't help anybody.

Being physically trapped and confined to the yard, we incurred so much stress on a daily basis. That stress was combated by boredom and those conflicting emotions bred instant storms for many inmates. I wanted my fifteen minutes on the phone to help me escape. I wanted that time to take my mind back home; back to my life and the ones I loved. Those fifteen minutes were my mental freedom so when I couldn't break free, my frustration levels would become compounded.

My friend faced similar problems as I did with his children's mother inspiring some of the arguments. I couldn't deal with the problems head on though. I was limited in my reactions but verbal communication didn't seem to work in my favor. I already knew that arguing with her would never get me anywhere. It would exacerbate the situation. I would feel trapped and powerless and end up yelling over the phone, allowing somebody else to drain me of my positive energy. That was a promise that I had made, and I owed to myself to keep; no one would be allowed to take my happiness from me, not even me.

I was caught in a dilemma. I needed to address a situation with my son's mother, but I was anxious that the conversation would not go well and that it might cause me to become upset. I was turning over a new leaf and did not want to lose my cool over the phone. My biggest fear was that I would say something that I might not want to, causing her to get upset and to keep me from hearing my son's voice throughout the rest of my stay here. If I wanted to make my girlfriend happy though, I knew that something needed to be done. I loved my son more than anything and I also loved my girlfriend, but this situation with my son's mother had to be addressed so that it wouldn't happen again. James repeatedly tried calming me down by repeating my own words.

"The tongue, brother. Listen, communicate and get your point across respectfully and intelligently" he'd repeat over and over trying to annoy me. "You don't have to be a condescending asshole just to get your point across," he continued, shaking his head in disbelief at me.

James thought I was blessed with the gift of attraction. He was amazed by the wealth of knowledge I possessed and attributed that knowledge as a bonus that attracted all inmates. No matter what color, gang or age, when I spoke, everyone listened. On the other hand, he also saw me to be slightly arrogant and a bit too serious at times. I didn't see myself as arrogant at all; well, maybe sometimes, but never without reason. I understood why he saw me to be serious because this is my life and my life is serious, or so I made it out to be. My life was not a joke to me and I make no mistakes about that. I was sitting in a prison cell so whoever wanted to continue viewing their life as a joke that was their choice; it wasn't mine. I continued to conduct myself as a business professional. I envisioned myself owning my own businesses and recognized that I had employees to manage and fires to put out. This would be a challenge but a CEO faces challenges every single day. In the end, I handled this challenge by communicating with my son's mother in a respectful way.

While there were problems in my life outside of the prison gates, there was not too much going on inside of those prison walls. We spent two days locked down for quarterly contraband searches. Lock-down was not a joke. The past days two days felt like an entire month. Boring was not even the word. With every movement restricted, there wasn't much else to do but to play cards, play dominoes, read books, and watch TV. The bathroom looked like a pigpen since inmates were smoking inside of it during the two days. They flung their cigarette butts all over the floor. The urinal had clogged up from cigarette butts but nobody cared about anything. It was every man for himself seeking his own way how to escape reality.

Staring at the man in the mirror, I made a vow to myself. I decided to take the rest of this journey on my own. I was tired of arguing every day, barking over the phone and belittling myself. If the person on the other line didn't see the beauty in me then it wasn't meant to be. It was easy for her to point out my flaws, but she could not see the light that was peering through. Nevertheless, the place I was in wasn't helping me permeate that light and it's easy to be blinded by the struggle. I was going to concentrate on myself and the environment that surrounded me. I was dealing with way too many components to mess up.

First thing I had to do was man-up and take responsibility for my life. I knew I had the mental strength and will to take this journey by myself. Now, I just had to show everybody else that as well. I was very appreciative of everything that had been done for me along the way, but arguing everyday was getting me nowhere. Maybe it was the fact that I was away and she missed me that was the problem. Maybe it was just time for us both to take some time apart or possibly even move on completely. Whatever the case, I was ready to take that step.

Waking up to yet another lock-down was not how I had planned on starting my day. The entire run was on edge. Everyone was tense as their every move was once again regulated. For some reason, my outlook was one of hope though. It was a new day and therefore, it was filled with endless possibilities. Even though I was restricted from going outdoors, I found myself in pursuit of the small blessings that could make my day beautiful. I guess being locked down got the best of me after a while as I found myself laying back in my bed with thoughts of my past racing through my head. I began thinking about times that I was out having fun and enjoying my life, even though I was a prodigal with my money. I spent my money as quickly as I made it, hoping to make it all back the next day. My cavalier attitude had to change. My new sense of financial literacy allowed me to realize that I had to embrace vulnerability; not just in matters of money but in relationship matters as well. To be truthful and honest, all the time was priceless and held a value most weren't even capable of understanding.

Inevitably, the haunting thoughts re-appeared. How was my girlfriend doing? How was my son? My heart crumbled without being able to see them and hold them tight. I knew that I had most definitely grown mentally during my journey and I was proud that I was continuing to mature in every way possible, even under the circumstances that I was in. In addition to the vow that I made to myself about always communicating properly with anyone, I also committed to a new decision. The conversation had to be positive and meaningful. Anything negative and futile would simply be dismissed. I was in prison. I was captive for the time being, but I was prepared to fight through those negative thought patterns I had created for myself as my own trap.

"The yard's open!" the CO shouted.

"Finally," I whispered to myself.

Everyone quickly got up and marched outside. I remained in bed, even though I could now move about. I guess I've always gone against the grain somewhat! I realized that what I liked was the option. I was accustomed to having the option of going outside and coming back in once I was ready. We were stripped of all power here so once that option of moving about freely was taken away too, it felt overwhelming.

"Tap! Tap! Tap! Rude Boy! Wake up. You still sleeping?" a familiar voice said to me.

I knew it had to be important because the prison rule was never to wake someone unless he had asked you prior. If you woke a sleeping inmate without being asked, the only acceptable reasons were: there was a riot occurring or officers were doing random searches. I pulled the sheets from over my face.

"What's up, OG?" I asked, wiping my eyes.

"We got you that bed move that you wanted," Big Chris, the Head of the Kinfolks explained.

"What? That's crazy. Are you serious?" I questioned him, making sure it wasn't some form of prank.

I was hoping this move would make my time a bit more comfortable. I was tired of top bunk. Jumping up and down all the time was brutal.

I jumped out of bed and went next door to my new building, Building 7. I found my bed space, which was a bottom bunk. I had been waiting for this for the last three months. You were only supposed to get a bottom bunk if you had been on that yard for six months. I had pulled a favor from my head due to my illegal business. I cleaned up my new bed space and moved my property over. I completed the move in two trips as I had everyone I knew help bring everything I owned. I hadn't met my new cellmate yet, but I didn't give much thought to it. I had a bottom bunk and that's all that mattered. I was happy to get away from all the bullshit in my old building. It was a different pace in my new run. It was mostly older inmates or inmates that were seasoned veterans or convicts.

These convicts were quieter than I had ever experienced before. Everyone did their jobs inside the run and the bathroom was always spotless. They were laid back, but I quicklyrealized a lot of movement was going on. I made my bed and decided to try out bottom bunk. One by one though, the very inmates I was hoping to get away from popped up. My neighboring cellmate's first question to me was why did I have so many visitors.

"Be careful with whatever it is you're doing. This place is full of snitches," Gustavo, my neighbor stated.

I nodded, implying that I had nothing to worry about. I hadn't done anything wrong so I had no reason to be concerned. On the contrary, I was trying to get away from the troublemakers in Building 6. I continued to brainwash myself, believing my own lies.

Gustavo was very prison intelligent. He understood the ins and outs or prison and he made a living from it. He was Cuban but was involved in a major gang. He was quiet until he was hungry.

"Jamaica! Jamaica! What you got over there, brother? I'm hungry," he yelled as if I wasn't right across from him.

I would hook him up as he became my lookout when the officers were inside the building, and when I wasn't home, he'd watch my store.

My cellmate was a brother mixed with Navaho Indian. He was tall and athletic and worked out every day. He was pissed that I got his bottom bunk. He had been here longer than I had and wanted to be moved down to the bottom bunk like he should. He didn't speak to me directly but would complain to Gustavo. Gus would tell me after the fact what he had said. Gus said I intimidated him because he had heard about me and he thought I was a bully. It didn't help either that I didn't speak a lot and most took it to mean I wasn't friendly. When his friends would come around, he would always be sure to tell them to keep it down and not to mess with my property. He would tell them that I was a no-nonsense type of guy. I would pretend that I was listening to music with my eyes closed but I was listening to every word they said. Gus taught me that trick;lListen with my eyes and see with my ears.

Prison was complicated but for every complication there was a lesson to be learnt. It was the only infallible way to avoid compounding problems.

I sat on my chair sorting out commissary that I had just collected from store. I felt a sudden tap on my shoulder, which made me feel very uneasy. I was usually very aware of my surroundings, which typically made it very difficult to startle me.

"Yo, Knowledge is looking everywhere for you," James said, grinning because of his successful sneak attack he played on me. I had always told him he would never get me like that but I had to laugh out loud, acknowledging that he had won. For a second I wondered about my brother YG. How was he doing?

"I'm coming. I'm so glad nobody knows where to find me since my move. I feel like I've moved out of the hood and into the suburbs," I said, grabbing an extra pair of socks to put on.

I grabbed a bottle of water and kicked my box under the bed as I walked out into the run. Upon exiting the building, a sudden draft of heat engulfed my entire body all at once. It felt as if I was cooking in a pizza oven. In just seconds, my clothes became so warm that they felt as if they were just ironed. I walked over to the basketball court and noticed that everyone was parting ways, saying what's up and showing me respect. I had become the new Kevin. I couldn't go anywhere and not be stopped and bothered.

I sat down on the bench underneath the Ramada, took off my shoes and doubled up my socks. As I looked up, my usual view was blocked by a minivan. Usually, the view was of a parking lot filled with cars. Just past the sprawling lot was another prison facility called Cheyenne. That was a Level Three yard. "What's that van doing around here? I've never seen it parked over there before," I said to Knowledge as I pulled my shoes on and stood up, a little interested in what was going on.

"That's for the PC niggas," he replied. "They must be getting moved today. That's why they have back-up so close. They're crazy if they think that everybody doesn't already know who they are anyways," he ended.

One of these such people had owed me fifty dollars and he owed others much more. I said nothing, dissolving the conversation as

I asked for the basketball. I started to shoot around a little as I waited for our game to start.

Knowledge was a brother, six foot one, from Tucson. He was a man of few words; spoke only when necessary. We became cool after playing dominoes together. Like most brothers on the yard, he was there on a murder charge. He had done nine years, so far, on a fourteen-year sentence. He was dark-skinned, displayed prison tattoos all over his upper body, and had been working out since he had been down. His chest was permanently pronounced from years of working out. He had a teardrop tattoo underneath his left eye. He knew that I didn't have much experience playing basketball but he wanted me on his team. He knew I had been a soccer player but I was big, tall, and fast so he asked me to join his team for a prison basketball tournament.

"Rude Boy, hey! We're going to play a 2,3 formation. You're going to be the big man in the middle at all times. Just watch out for the three-second violation in the paint and just play your game and stay big," he finalized his pep talk.

"Aright, my G. Just talk to me during the game," I replied, walking into the circle for the jump ball.

Prison basketball is very different from regular basketball. We all mouthed off to each other, talking about how much we weighed when we scored a bucket. Dirty South, my barber from Arkansas, was playing for the opposite team. He and SG went at it, going back and forth. SG fell on the hard concrete a few times because Dirty South pushed him. Dirty had done eleven years for attempted murder and aggravated assault and was about to go home in two weeks.

Nevertheless, that changed nothing for him. He and SG were up in each other's faces every possession. They looked like they were two pit-bulls, ready to fight. All I could imagine was when two dogs were being restrained by their owners but they were able to get just close enough so that they could each intimidate the other to the best of their ability. Both continued to swear on their gangs and made it clear that they were 'about the business', which was prison talk meaning they were down for anything.

Our game went into overtime as the regulation time ended in a tie. The game had an impenetrable intensity due to the rivalry between Dirty South and SG. We lost though, by one single point in overtime. Knowledge complimented me on my efforts, as the other team had to foul me in the end of the game. I kept picking up all of the rebounds but I was poor at free throws. As the game ended, I realized that the yard had closed so I ran across the softball field to grab a tray of food that Wayne had prepared.

Wayne was the newest Jamaican on the yard and ever since he got here, he had been the new chef. I would bring him commissary but I would also bring him other ingredients that were not typically available on the yard. I had cabbage, onions, carrots, and bell peppers. These were delicacies. I would either buy it from the kitchen workers or I would buy it from inmates that got them in their KOSHER diet trays. Wayne had recently arrived but he didn't take long to get used to the yard. He had received the Jamaican welcome. He had everything the day he arrived. He had done time in the New York prison system and thus was more experienced in cooking with commissary items than I had been. I walked into the run to find him watching TV next to a tray that was wrapped in plastic wrap. He handed me the tray then asked, "Did you win? I saw you doing your thing. I didn't know that you played basketball. I see you Patrick Ewing," he smirked and dapped me up at the same time.

"I don't really play but Knowledge had asked me to. It's not like I have anything else going on so I might as well kill some time," I replied. "Thanks again Brother. I'm starving," I said as I dapped him again and turned around to run back home. I needed to get out of the run before the COs gave me ticket.

Wayne had changed the game completely. I no longer needed anyone to send money to get spice. I sent his daughter's mom the money to buy the product and take the ride to visit him. He'd tell her the spot to leave it at. He was allowed to work outside the fences. I was forbidden because of my immigration detainer and he wasn't. He was more of a mix between me and Kevin. A little flashy but jovial and but don't get him mad.

Wayne had made burritos for dinner. He made them with tuna, chicken, jalapeño peppers, noodles, rice, cheese and jalapeño pretzels that were all wrapped up inside of a tortilla. On the side, there was some cabbage that was sautéed with bell peppers and carrots. The plastic wrap covered the food but it was not strong enough to mask the scent of one of my most favorite, authentically Jamaican side dishes. I gave Mr. McGee one of the burritos and saved the rest for after I completed my shower. I bought a cup of ice, made some lemonade, and enjoyed my meal. It was delicious and well needed. The food tasted so good that it didn't seem like it had been made from prison commissary items. I brushed my teeth and then read for a bit, before turning my TV on and allowing the tension to subside in my body as I took comfort in the normalcy of my night, even if it was only for a brief moment.

Basketball, softball, and soccer were the only games played that were seen by the public eye. Inmates had other games running that were not quite so obvious. These games were driven by profit, where commissary was the hard cash. It was played in the form of "running store" where inmates would loan out commissary items and charge anywhere from 25-50% interest to their customers. These stores would generate so much income or commissary, that their owners would have to spread out their inventory so as to prevent the COs from catching on and taking it all. Inmate stores would sell food boxes to fellow inmates in exchange for cash that was to be sent to somebody back home or put into their account. The store would give you a deal of 20% in extra commissary for any amount of money that they received over a $100. If $100 were sent to a store, then in turn, you would receive $120 of commissary. Inmates also hustled by cleaning houses, cleaning shoes, doing laundry and by acting as runners for the store and handing out lists of debt and collecting money when it was due. When the rations of food you were given were barely enough for a grown man to survive on, these were the types of things you had to do to stay alive in prison.

Gambling generated another source of income for inmates. The game day sports spread was controlled by my Jamaican partner, who was fourteen years my senior. I would always seek out his advice on any play action that I decided to run. Besides the spread run on basketball and football, we also had Heads Up bets that were placed between two inmates. There was no house to collect on for this bet. Someone was declared a winner and either you paid them or you'd fight. Another means of making money was playing Squares. It was a true gamble as it was based on random selection. An inmate could buy a square, costing anywhere from sixty cents to five dollars, but that so-called square was randomly chosen or placed on a numbered chart. The winner was determined by the score of the game, which ultimately correlated with a square on the chart. The house, or the person in control of the squares, collected 20% of all of the bets placed. Since the final payout was 80%, he was guaranteed to make some money.

OG Rasta was the prison lawyer. He charged inmates to look into their cases. He would search for any loopholes in hopes of reducing sentences, determining how and when to file motions or appeals and would also help in attempting to reduce or even drop restitution orders. He would also help inmates file their paperwork with the prison after they received tickets for a violation. As with lawyers on the outside, his services weren't cheap. He had been in prison for so many years that he had learned to use his education and intelligence for the good of all. He became so knowledgeable about the systems and all of its loopholes that he was indispensable to the inmates inside. He had a vast knowledge of creating recipes from the little ingredients we were given. He made the best food on the yard and his prison 'hooch' (alcohol) was the best.

Drugs were the most lucrative business on the inside. The drug of choice for inmates who used was called Spice. Spice was a chemically based drug whose high was similar to that of ingesting marijuana. It was much stronger and much more dangerous. It had previously been sold legally on the streets but upon realizing its potency, it had been banned. Inmates gravitated to Spice over other drugs because it was not detected in prison drug tests. While marijuana, heroin, and cocaine would test positive in urine tests, for some reason the chemical makeup of Spice did not yet register, so inmates could get away with it. When Spice hit the yard, it created a hustler's frenzy like no other. One single ounce of Spice went for $150-$250 dollars on the street but you would find that same ounce for anywhere from $500 to even a $1000 in prison. Ounces were broken down into clips. A clip sold for twenty-five dollars and a clip would be broken down into boxes that ranged from four to six dollars a piece, depending on availability. One clip could fetch you anywhere from fifteen to twenty boxes, provided that the size and quality of the clip were good. If a whole ounce was broken down, you could make thousands.

A good batch drove the inmates wild and this would just increase the demand even more. This was good for making money but you attracted the wrong eyes. When inmates 'fell out' or had seizures, your product was more sought after but the person with the product was wanted by the police. Kevin was rolled up for his high-quality product. Menace had been rolled-up for the same thing and Slim was the latest victim. One thing Menace and Slim had in common was they smoked themselves so they would act out of character and slip up. Slim was written up twice as he was caught getting head in visitation from them tapping his phones. Kevin, a. true Jamaican was very boisterous and always challenged the Police. I was reserved, played sports, worked out, read books, and collected a whole bunch of commissary. Even though I was collecting commissary, I still shopped from the store to have receipts of my purchases. With anything else, Spice brought great reward but also brought great risk. Prison authorities constantly targeted dealers and they rose to prison-fame amongst the inmate population.

How do you get Spice into the prison you might ask? Many methods can be used but the most popular was Keistering. Keistering was using the anal cavity to smuggle drugs. The person smuggling the drugs in was usually given a 25% cut of the price of his shipment but he risked a lot, as this method was very dangerous.

When inmates found themselves in debt, whether they owed other inmates for Spice or they owed money to stores, the trend was to PC up and go into protective custody. Prison authorities were tiring of this trend so they began targeting those that were responsible for the illegal businesses. Their most recent victim was OG Rod. Every week, there was a sting operation. Rod was a cool brother but he smoked too. He was doing twenty-six years for murder. He had twenty-three years down so far. Rod didn't sell Spice but he did have it brought in for his own personal use. He would smoke and then just go lay in his bed. He never bothered anybody and nobody ever bothered him. He recently got married and had only six months until he was released. As he explained it to me, he smoked Spice to get through the remainder of his time. He had so much pressure on him to succeed and that consumed his mind twenty-four hours a day, seven days a week. With all that anxiety and emotion, one can easily be overwhelmed and turn to drugs for relaxation.

"I have a wife now, Rude Boy," Rod explained. "When I get out, it won't just be me that I'll be responsible for. I have to think about somebody else too."

He looked deep into my eyes as he expressed his fears. His eyes drooped from his high.

"I have six months and I'm back out on the streets. Every day I think about the person's life I took back in 1991. He had two sons that are men now that probably want to kill me." He paused and stroked his facial hair as he pondered on his past that was about to collide with his future. "I ain't going to let anyone kill me, so what am I to do? I'm not leaving Phoenix, so I have to just deal with all this bullshit. When I smoke Spice, I'm happy. I don't have to think about any of that bull shit," he reasoned.

He was high but he spoke the truth so I listened and he continued to confide in me as if I were his therapist. He clearly had a lot weighing on his mind and he needed to vent. All that I could do for him was listen. He was set to face a lot of real-life circumstances once he was released and those thoughts were terrifying him. A thought crossed my mind of YG as I listened to Rod speaking. He repeated YG's famous saying, "You're either going to be the sheep or the wolf. You have to decide."

Having a hustle was very important for those who didn't have any money on their books. Prison jobs paid fifteen cents an hour; that meant $6 every two weeks.

There's not too much you can do to survive on $6 a week anywhere. To supplement this, inmates would play the role of middlemen, runners, and supply storage for store holders. The survival instinct was human nature. It was life on the streets in its upgraded version. If an inmate's job couldn't adequately support them then they would have to find something else to sustain them. In prison, your options are highly restricted so hustling became a means of survival for some. For others, hustling was only something that they used to occupy their time as days dragged on. In a backwards and twisted way, that was the only real support prison provided. It was a method strategically created to break relationships and continue isolation that would further push you down a dark, sordid, and never-ending road. Get far enough and you could lose yourself. This dark life gave some men a meaningless purpose in this confined rat race. Those that say prisons are meant to punish and rehabilitate, plain and simply know nothing about prison. Prisons perpetuate a cycle. That's all they force, that's all they teach, and that's all they allow.

Living in this small community, I finally came to understand what YG, Simpson, and Sanchez had once spoken about. I understood because I experienced the hopelessness and the poverty physically and mentally. I lived it. Everyone wants to be somebody in life. Even a person born in the ghetto wants to feel important. The quickest way for most was to be feared, sell drugs, and call it a come up. At the end of the day, they were now important and fulfilled a basic need in life so it was all good. Most were willing to lose their life for the taste of such a feeling. The constant stress and pressure that bills, struggle, and fear amass changed people. Prison was an environment of extremes. Every part of your being is continually tested; physically, emotionally, and mentally. One must always be on-guard, even when sleeping. The toll that this takes on your body and mind when they have already been stretched past the point of human acceptance is intolerable. Society dictates that prisoners stand a fifty percent chance of rehabilitation upon release. I would love to see where those fifty percent came from. The word rehabilitation wasn't even in the dictionary here. A repeat offender tore it out. There were two options in prison: you were either nothing or you were the best. You either hustled or you starved. Learn or die.

It just didn't make sense. What were your chances when you left prison and were stereotyped and biased against? Rejected by job after job and left to fend for yourself? The very people you want to get away from become your lifeline. A man that is forced to live in poverty and exposed to drug dealing becomes his life. That's all he knows and therefore, that is what he is destined to become. Most had endured the struggle and they were prepared to go back to the same thing, as support in legal ventures wasn't welcoming. The cruel teacher that life is just kept testing inmates and gave the lesson after. By then, most didn't appreciate it so among repeat offenders the thought of prison as a punishment or discipline was tabooed.

There was really no way to stay out of the mix if you had something that everyone wanted. I decided that it really was time for me to quit all forms of the game completely after James got rolled-up to another yard. He had left for Kingman Correctional Facility after a massive race riot had taken place over the 4th of July weekend. The brothers had started the riot and they were all taken to the hole. The Warden from Yuma sent brothers over to fill up Kingman as all the brothers there would be shipped out to new facilities. Nine COs had been hospitalized, along with four inmates. The prisoners started the riot as a means of protesting the way they were treated and the conditions under which they were forced to live in. Ultimately, the damage to Kingman was so extensive that almost 1,200 inmates had to be moved to a new location.

Over the weekend, I had received a letter from my sister that informed me of an immigration hold that was placed on me because of my status in the US as a Legal Permanent Resident versus that of a citizen. If I ever needed a wakeup call, this was it. Time is money and serving time in prison meant that I was bankrupt. The fact that I would have to deal with an immigration case upon completing my sentence terrified me, to say the least. How could I ever handle being away from my son? What about my girlfriend? And the life that I had grown accustomed to living? All of the money in the world meant nothing to me anymore; all I wanted to do was to be with my son and my girlfriend. I had been away for so long already. I didn't want to be shipped off to another country. Never in my life had I felt so low. I felt utterly defeated. Nothing could ease the stress that I was feeling and the natural confines of prison surely didn't help. I spent the entire day laying in my bed and watching TV. The television might as well have watched me though, because my mind was numb and completely incapable of understanding anything at all during those never-ending moments.

Prison isn't what people expect it to be. Even beyond the fact that you are physically held captive, prison imposes things on you that no human being should ever have to endure. Men are forced to participate in the most degrading of circumstances; stripping down to nothing, bending over and spreading your legs for inspection by COs, being forced to use the bathroom in a room the size of a hotel room but that is filled with 16 other prisoners mere inches away.

Showering was a different story. Every stall was separated by shower curtains, allowing for some privacy. On a day like today, when I was feeling down, the shower was always the place that I found myself seeking comfort. It was the only place that you could truly find privacy and be alone with your thoughts. I would shower three times in one day sometimes. It relaxed me and allowed me to feel like an actual human being, even if only for a moment. These showers made me do a lot of thinking about my girlfriend. Even though I appreciated her support, I decided I would write her a letter to explain some of the thoughts I'd been having lately. Prison was 100% mental to me. There was nothing but pure mental struggle involved in waking up to the same routine every single day, to the same people, the same sweltering sun, the same bland and nameless food and all of the same bullshit in between.

I began my letter by expressing my undying gratitude for all that she had done for me. She had constantly put money on the phone so I could call her, she picked up my every call and allowed me the chance to mentally escape – even if only for a few minutes a day. Lately, however, I felt like she had just been going through the motions. She was not my happy girlfriend that I was used to and what pained me was that I had no doubt I was the cause of that. Being incarcerated not only affected me but it also affected my loved ones. I had been selfish for the majority of our relationship but I didn't want her to be with me if it meant that she was going to be unhappy. I loved her too much to drag her through this rollercoaster of emotions. If walking away from me would make her feel better, then I would take the rest of this journey alone.

I contemplated what I was doing for a while after writing my letter and mailing it off. On one hand, I felt like writing that letter was the right thing to do. On the other, she said she wanted to be there for me so I felt like I shouldn't question her and was being a bit negative. It's also possible that all the stories I've heard on the yard really got in my head. Everyone seemed to have a story about a wife or a girlfriend that left them once they were locked up. Whatever my motivation was for writing that letter, I was only hoping she would reply with a sincere desire to make this work. It would be one thing to part ways under normal circumstances, while living on the outside. Leaving somebody while they are in prison though could be detrimental to a person's survival.

I started to feel the impact of my letter even before she wrote me back. I became more aggressive, almost boisterous, to the point of picking a fight, but nobody bit the bait. They showed care and took time to find out what was wrong with me. They had never seen me acting like this before. I knew it was just one of those days, as just the day before I had been so positive. I continuously tried to find that place where I could be mentally positive so that I could relax my mind, but I searched to no avail. I had days like this on the outside where I would go to the lake to escape. I would sit and let my mind run free. The water and the animals that were going about their business would entrance me. Outside of my house were boulders that my son always called "Daddy's rocks." These rocks were another little sanctuary of mine. If neither of those places would allow me to escape, then I would usually take a drive to someplace new, admiring the beauty and opportunity that the outside world had to offer.

My neighbor, Herb, was an interesting man. He had written a *New York Times* Best Seller and had previously owned an investment firm. He came to prison on a fraud charge. He will be the first to tell you that, although he did not commit the crime he was accused of, he did commit other crimes. He had lost nine and a half million dollars of investors' money in an effort to develop real estate in Mexico. Prior to his downfall, Herb had been a very successful businessman. He frequently spoke to large audiences on his passion and his success and was a very convincing and charismatic man. Herb was not your typical Jewish man. He was a slick talker; he quickly sized people up and spent most of his days busy, as he continued on with his writing.

Herb was about six foot two, with a straight and pointed nose,s and had a head full of grey hair that was held tightly on to a remaining patch of black hair in the back. He was always clean-shaven and he had an air of confidence about him that was unusual to see in these parts. One thing that I noticed was that he had an overabundance of body hair on him, but that didn't seem to keep the women away as he professed that he had been with over 800 women in his lifetime. He had been married twice but not surprisingly, both women had divorced him due to infidelity. He had three children; one from his first marriage and two from his second. His children were all very successful, according to society's definition of what success entails. He was highly analytical when it came to life, people, relationships and himself. In spite of, or maybe because of, all these self-proclaimed successes, Herb was very self-loathing.

Herb trusted no woman and claimed that he has never been jealous of either of his wives throughout the course of their respective relationships. Although that seemed odd to me, it was not my position to question another man's personal feelings. His trust issues were a direct consequence of his relationship with his father, whom he called a psychopath. His stepfather had abused him so badly and yet his mother did nothing to stop him. While his stepfather was the true abuser, he blamed his actions on his mother's failure to protect her child. This seemed to be the basis for which he built his distrust of the women in his life. Herb was a highly intelligent man, to say the least. As with most of the inmates in prison though, I found myself often questioning many of his views on life.

"Nobody thinks about you, Jamaica," he would say. "Don't you worry about what others think. They think nothing of you but they think of themselves. They think about what they can get from you. That's all."

I do admit that I often did find that to be the case. His story of the Zen Master was another story that I liked for the simple reason that good and bad both occur in life. In the end though, good can come to mean bad and bad can come to mean good. As my mother always said, "Time is the master for everything." He analyzed me and always told me that I was a chronic over-thinker. He also told me that I was talented but that I held anger inside. He recommended that I take anger management classes upon my release.

"I must say that in being as big as you are and as angry as you can be, I would be scared of you if I didn't know you. I would hate to see what you would do to somebody that pissed you off. You are charismatic but you are also very angry. You are a great person, Jamaica, and you have that accent going for you too! But I still sense that anger and we need to do something about that," he would always say, with a twinkle in his green eyes as he gazed out the window.

Herb believed that control issues drove my anger. He saw that I always tried to control my environment and to him, control was just an illusion. It was his belief that until I recognized that as a fact, I would always remain an angry, talented, over thinker. Herb had the same routine every day. He would wake up at 5:30am and would write for a few hours, working on his novels and murder mystery books that he was creating. He watched a bit of television, relaxed on his bunk in between meals, and then watched the cooking channel that Rosa hosted in the evening. He would socialize for a while before dinner and then after he would write again, before watching tv and retiring to his bunk to sleep. Every day since he had lived next to me, he had practiced this same routine. He invested his time wisely into his endeavors and this was a characteristic of his that I admired and always worked to emulate.

I hadn't been in the best of moods for the past two days, so I remained in bed longer than usual. I did not sleep my day away but rather I invested some time into myself. I spent the day reading entrepreneurial magazines, financial investment books, and talking to Herb. Our conversation turned into one that was very interesting, as we discussed the masks that everyone wears. It all started as I had to speak to my cellmate about a consistent issue. I told him that he was playing with other inmates too much around our bunk space. I didn't like that and one person specifically: Cookie! The conversation blossomed into a more intellectual topic about a book that I was working on and the fact that everybody walks around here with their chest poked out, boasting about being a gangster and a killer. I told him that I was no killer and I certainly don't claim to be. Herb overheard our conversation and joined in. His viewpoint was that everybody wears a mask and that they live in constant fear that people will eventually figure them out for the fraud that they are underneath.

He carried the conversation further into his own experiences and spoke about an instance where he was at an Alcoholics Anonymous meeting that was being conducted by a well-known therapist, up in the Hollywood Hills. The therapist's multimillion-dollar home was used as the meeting location. It was an ideal venue, as it almost felt as if you could reach the iconic "hills" sign and the views from the living room were breathtaking. He met actors, actresses, rappers, models, business moguls and other well-known and talented individuals. Each of these people lived a life that was idolized by thousands, if not millions, all across the world. They lived the lives of fame and luxury and for all intents and purposes, they had it all. Another thing that they all had though, was the shared and constant fear that either they might lose their job at any given moment or that they would not be able to maintain the lifestyle that they had become accustomed to living. Many also complained that they had lost it all and they were wallowing in a pit of depression. Tears were a highly popular common denominator amongst all of the meeting's participants, no matter their level of success in life.

A commotion suddenly ensued at the entrance of the run, causing us to turn our attention to the ruckus. I stood up and realized that it was a group of brothers making all the noise. It was Big Chris, the Head for the brothers, followed by other inmates that ran with the Southside gang. Seconds after, Black came in and slammed the door, shouting and cursing at Chris. He wanted a one-on-one fight. Cervantes, the CO who was working at the time, stood at five feet two and probably weighed 120 pounds. She was paled skinned and very beautiful. Her cheeks were always red and her blush line from her makeup was flawless. Her work boots weren't the typical ugly soldier type. Hers were Nike with a slightly pink swoosh. Her outfits were well-pressed and her pants pulled all the way up to her belly button made sure her ass and her front print were prominent. Her mouse-like female voice was very distinct as she spoke out loud, "C'mon, this is crazy."

She was frozen and dumbstruck. COs ran in quickly after and threatened to pepper spray the entire run. Big Chris held his big paws in the air and repeatedly told them not to spray him, as he was not engaging in any physical conflict. I realized after that it had been a Southside *vs.* Westside city-gang conflict that had erupted. I tried to fit the pieces as both gangs ran together because they were all Crips. From what I could gather, Big Chris had punched Black and he fell to the ground and hit his head. The immediate swollen scar on the side of his face supported this. He yelled arguing with the brothers that tried to calm him down as he brushed his sand-covered hair. It was over something Black uttered in Big Chris's presence. It was never repeated to me nor was I interested.

It all died down after a host of COs separated the two gangs. They handcuffed Black and immediately closed the yard down. The Kinfolks were beginning to get a bad rep. We had caused one prison to lock down, caused a riot in another, and now there was a gang riot ensuing between the Southside and the Westside gang. By this time all the Kinfolks were on the yard. Nobody wanted to go inside as the tension ran thick. After much persuading by the COs and the Warden, however, everybody made their way back in. The whole lockdown had ruined my plans. Wayne had been cooking some fresh vegetables and chicken I had just purchased. I had not eaten and planned on enjoying this meal. I had tried calling my girlfriend earlier in the day but didn't get her so I was waiting until right before the yard closed for the evening to try calling her again. It was too late now to make that phone call but I was going to attempt to get my meal. That quickly proved futile. Out of nowhere, I found myself being thrown up against the side of the building, thoroughly searched and then given a ticket because I was outside during lockdown.

The CO was an asshole. Everyone that knew me knew that I was a humble individual. I always made sure I was polite to the officers and I never did anything to stir the pot or to make them upset. Any other officer would have simply warned me verbally if they realized I was doing something out of line, but not this guy; he felt like he had something to prove.

Oftentimes, COs would bring their troubles from home to work. I could tell someone had pissed him off prior because there was no way he was supposed to be so mad from me being out of place. Some officers just loved the power they were given once they set foot on the yard. They were in charge of men and many weren't even in charge of their own homes. Employees brought their problems to work with them all the time; but not when you work in a prison. Prison had enough problems already; it certainly didn't need anymore. It was usually pretty easy to gauge when a CO is having one of those days. Some inmates will sense that and try to get under their skin. I never bothered them.

As a matter of fact, when I could generally tell something was wrong, I would avoid them completely. I typically don't even speak to them unless they spoke to me. That included the female officers as well that were vacillating and fickle. It was just best to avoid since they all knew what I was doing but couldn't prove it.

The whole saga had played out between Big Chris and Black. Big Chris was still the Head and Black was sent to a different yard. The yard was subsequently closed down and was back to controlled movement. All the officers were out and walked about on high alert.

By two o'clock the next day, things were finally back to normal as the yard reopened and the two sides were able to get together to discuss the issue at hand. It was quickly resolved, as Black had led the COs into the run, violating the inmate code. If he had remained on the yard, he quickly would have received a second ass-whopping. A conversation taking place between Big Chris, the leader of the South Side Gang, and Emit, the leader on the yard for the West Side City Gang, was interrupted by Rod, who was always the prison politician.

"Whether or not a brother is right, I would ride for another brother in a racial dispute - bottom line," Rod said, his voice echoing over everyone else around him. "What I don't like to see is when brothers choose sides when brothers have issues amongst themselves. Let them go to the bathroom and handle their issues like men. When people have a domestic dispute but start banging their gangs, then you are going to pick up for your boy," he paused and pointed at a South Sider. "I am going to ride for my boy because you drew a line. I have no choice but to ride for my hood because that's what I bang. That's exactly the problem. There should be no sides taken. We should all let the domestic shit be handled between those two bothers. Nobody gets involved unless it's an issue with another race. That's the way that I was cut up by the system. I know that a lot has changed but those simple rules should at least be understood." He ended his rant and walked away from the group, sitting next to me on the wall, under the phone booths.

"Jamaica! Aye, Rude Boy - back in my days, shit was much more structured. Today these youngsters come off the streets with that banging shit and they bring it inside of here. Back in the day, you left all that gang shit at the door. We are the minority in here so we have to have each other's back. Half of these little negroes wouldn't survive their first two weeks in the penitentiary back in the 80's. You walked through the gates back then and you were tested every day. You had to have heart. A big stature meant nothing. I've seen big-ass niggas PC-up because they can't handle it. I've witnessed it all; all of the wildest shit you can imagine. I've set off a riot and then I've been involved in over seven more since then.

Sometimes you find out that the dudes you expect to be next to you aren't who they claim to be at all. Heart! Niggas had heart! This new generation needs more of that! Niggas need to be tested. Prison is not like the penitentiary I knew. It is commercialized for political gains so the state and its investors can reap their benefits. Back then, we were convicts. These new niggas today are inmates. It was convicts against the COs. Them against us; us against them. Not us against ourselves. That shit doesn't even look right. It hurt me in my heart.

Deep inside of my heart, Jamaica," he ended, using his index finger to poke at the left side of his chest.

It was clear that this issue touched him deeply. It angered and saddened him to his core to see his own people so divided. Like everything else in the world, prisons had evolved. Convicts evolved and got better at their trade. They found many different ways to smuggle in contraband and consequently, the COs found more advanced technology in hopes of keeping ahead of these methodologies. Prison education has also changed. Prisons offer a wide variety of programs that range from GED classes, to college courses, to AA programs, drug treatment classes, methadone clinics, construction engineering, electrical programs and when you are down to only months remaining in your sentence, there are re-entry programs that are offered to help assist in the transition process of going home. So much more than simply the attitude of prisoners had changed throughout the generational evolution, however. The highly controversial private prison industry has grown at an alarmingly high rate and now houses nearly twenty percent of prisoners in the system.

These prisons are being used to generate income for areas that lack opportunity. Typically, the notion is valid that bringing big business to a struggling area will create jobs and opportunity, thus bolstering the regional economy. That same notion cannot apply when people's lives are at stake, though. Thousands of immigrants are now being housed at these private prisons across the country, as immigration detention centers are sickeningly overcrowded. Prisoner's sentences and immigrant's detention stays are being extended on average, as private prisons are capitalizing on human lives. Private prisons are quickly becoming one of the most secure investments in today's world, with the CEO of the Geo Group grossing $22 million dollars over a four-year timespan. These facilities are run under deplorable, inhumane conditions, with an increasingly high staff turnover rate and a dangerous lack of training. Together, these human atrocities add up to such significant cost-savings that the resulting profit that executives accrue could support an entire town.

Prisons no longer served edible food, nor did they care for the betterment of the inmate. Prisons, as with all other evolving industries today, are purely profit-driven. Where is the line though, when human lives are the goods that are sold? Bed-space quotas abound in nearly every prison across America, with those numbers being the primary decision-making factor in immigration detention centers and prisons. While every individual's perception is different, it seems my vision of the American Dream was slightly skewed. My American Dream involved opportunity, choice, and freedoms. Now, I'm seeing that this American Dream that so many strive for depends on the ability to fill quotas.

What have I learned? Never settle. Never let where you are decide your future. Never let your circumstances label you. Work on your being, from your core. Invest in yourself.

Strip yourself. Strip yourself of all expectation, all pretense. Strip yourself of everything you have ever known, desired and worked for. Eliminate all influencing factors, take a step away and view yourself in raw form. Then, and only then, will you have the ability to become reunited with your real and true self. You control your happiness and I speak from experience when I say that it is better to be happy than to insist on being right. Life throws us to the ground. It steps on us. You may even get run over! But never let the fear of striking out stop you from taking a swing at the ball. Pursue your dream. Do not wait for the right opportunity because there will always be a reason that the timing may not be perfect.

Create your own opportunity. Recognize the opportunity in

your situation. If opportunity can be found in prison, then trust me when I say that opportunity can be found anywhere.

My complete and total change occurred after I realized what I really wanted in my life. I realized what I really needed. I needed security, comfort, family, and great health. This was my true wealth. Life in prison guaranteed that none of those needs would be met. I was separated from my family and prison life was as far from secure and comfortable as you could imagine.

Reading books is easy. Motivational speakers can be powerful, yet their words fade if you listen but didn't absorb. You can tell yourself that you are going to make a change but when a true change takes place, it is not even thought about it is put into action. It took me twenty-six years of life to realize that talking was nothing; doing was where the magic could be found. I went through high school, graduated college, got married, and created a blessing in our son; I've succeeded, I've failed and I've been imprisoned. Ultimately, what it took to wake me up was to be totally and utterly alone with my thoughts and that's how I learned to live my change.

I found myself in a place of chaos; a place that at any given moment could turn into horror. Nevertheless, I found solace and hope. I thanked my family and true friends that stood by my side unconditionally. It is through their commitment and support that I found inspiration to survive. I had conquered myself and triumphed over the loneliest times of my life. This is my prison story - **#298706**.

This is not a fairy tale with perfect endings. I had grown accustomed to my surroundings. I was pushing my boundaries of learning. I began to see life differently but fell right back into my old pattern. I wondered why an old friend always told me that was why pencils came with erasers. I was bound to make mistakes and mistakes I had made, but there was no eraser. I found myself saying all the right things but engulfed with a resentful attitude. I hated my environment. I hated how my girlfriend made me feel over the phone. I hated that I couldn't take my son to school and pick him up after. I hated that I couldn't even promise him we'd go to the park on the weekends. My attitude changed my perception on everything. I knew what to do but just couldn't get around to doing it. I wanted to change the world but the small world of prison was changing me. Maybe my girlfriend was right.

Maybe it was just jail talk. Like she said, "Everybody that goes to prison either say they have changed or they've found God." The structure I was building internally had toppled over. There wasn't a firm foundation and the smallest of winds toppled everything I had worked on, returning me to my old self.

The sun shone directly over my bed. It was the heart of summer. Monsoons would hit and in minutes the sun would still be penetrating the soil with its 120 degrees heat. It was a risk to step outside. In matter of minutes, you were sweating profusely. Using the phones for fifteen minutes meant you got up and you were drenched in sweat. I had switched my workouts from mornings to afternoons when the sun was set. It was still incredibly hot and humid but it was more bearable. It was my nine-month anniversary and so much had happened over the last months.

Wayne's daughter, Wynter was born. He was a happy man but sad at the same time. He couldn't see her until she was three months when she would have gotten her first sets of vaccinations. My conversations with my girlfriend had taken a turn for the worst. We were arguing and I was told continuously that the only reason I hadn't done anything new to piss her off was because I was confined behind bars. She was right; I would have been messing up; but who didn't? At least when I messed up, I would fix it and I realized that's what she wanted me to do. This time I had prison to deal with and couldn't fix a thing other than myself. Could this be the possible solution? I felt worse when she cried over the phone. I knew I was putting her through hell. Being locked up in prison wasn't only affecting me but it was affecting her just as much.

Wayne and I were killing the game. We were flooding the yard with the best spice and we were controlling everything. We had so much commissary we didn't have enough space to hide it. Green Eyes and Big Chris had given us a few ideas and secrets of their own. Selling Spice on the weekends was less risky because the investigating unit didn't come in on weekends. By Monday though, they would be all over the yard trying to figure out who had what. I had gotten into a few situations myself. The biggest one was with California Eses that had the yard locked down for days because it almost resulted in a riot between them and us. Wayne and I had also lost some Spice because of Sticks. We had to discipline him and set him straight. He made stupid decisions after I had told him exactly what to do.

Then after it all, I walked into the bathroom later than usual from finishing up a book I was reading to find two men in one bathroom stall and another on guard duty or "holding point" in prison language. I immediately got boisterous and left to use the bathroom at the other end. Needless to say, we were walking on egg shells for days until they were both disciplined by their own race, the Chicanos.

After these events, Wayne and I had to lay low. I was in the Investigator Office being questioned about Spice, then tested for drugs through UAs three times in a week. They came and also searched my bed and commissary. They found nothing but we knew they were on to us. They were relentless in their efforts and kept me on my toes. Someone was giving up information. We were doing everything we were supposed to. I knew if one person could help us it was Big Chris. I decided to pay him a visit.

"What's up, OG?" I distracted his attention from his television.

"Good, Youngin," he answered.

I gave him a handshake and dropped a clip into his hands. He slipped his hands into his pockets and smiled.

"Boy, look at you. When you just got here, you barely talked and did nothing but mind your own business. Now, you Slick Rick," he laughed. My bribe worked as he continued, "Chuckie got caught and he told them people in SS he got Spice from the Jamaicans." He paused. "Young boy! You're smart but never take these people for fools. They don't have to get you with anything as you've witnessed with Kevin. These people aren't fools so be careful. Now I'm going to put this in the air. Thanks for looking out," he ended, walking off to the bathroom.

He was a monster of a man. He had done over fifteen years in prison. He stood six foot five and weighed over three hundred and sixty pounds. He never gave me wrong advice before; just a few selfish ones. I got back to Wayne and decided we would chill out for a bit. It was getting late so I decided to call my girlfriend.

"Do you know how many guys want to be with me and you treat me like nothing? How would you feel if you came home and I was pregnant?" she yelled at me over the phone.

The question she asked lit a fuse inside of me that would not let out. I grew angrier by the second. I couldn't believe what she just said to me. You had to have sex to get pregnant. Was this what she was telling me? I asked her if she was and she denied my assumptions. I had to take a few days' break from using the phones. My conversations weren't getting any better but rather much worse. I called her after a few days in hopes that everything had cooled down. I was not ready for what I was about to hear. "Whether you call me or not you don't change anything about my day," she scolded me.

I listened and carried on the conversation. As the operator intervened and told us we had one minute remaining, I felt saved. I sat at the phone booth and looked up at the dark clouds blowing from Mexico heading towards us.

I gazed and thought to myself, what was I doing? What else did she have to say to me for me to get the picture? She wasn't even asking me what I thought but more worried what people in her hometown would say about her. I was starting to see the picture clearly. She was already detached. She had moved on and didn't need my permission. What was I doing to myself? Hadn't I tortured myself enough prolonging the arguments. For the first time, it was clear and I knew what I had to do. I had to detach myself from all the negativity that surrounded me. I wrote her a lengthy letter and explained where I was mentally. I went to bed late and woke up early to drop off my mail.

I decided to wake up Wayne so we could workout. He was surprised I wanted to work out because it was our day off, plus it was already 110 degrees. I needed to do something physical rather than bash someone's head in. He understood without words explaining the circumstance. Something was bothering me. I worked out like a maniac and got a good pump in. The whole time I was in my head. I hadn't realized we had been working out for hours until the breakfast line was gone and the Officer yelled over the monitors that the dining hall was closed. We both decided we were going to cook for ourselves and stopped to relax by the phones. I made a quick phone call that ended in two minutes. I wished her the best and it was all over. I felt at ease. I could tell Wayne was stunned by the conversation.

Thick, dark clouds danced ominously across the evening sky. The sun played a tantalizing game of hide and seek. It was the middle of monsoon season yet not a drop of rain had visited the soil. A few months had passed – nine to be exact. I asked myself, "Why do you love her so much?" *Was it her look? Her slender, athletic body with those sexy dimples perched just over her immaculately tight butt? Was it her youthful qualities? Because those were sure to eventually fade. Her blessings would be taken and that beautifully sculpted face would start to droop, her flowing black hair would turn to ashy-gray. I must have seen the true little girl inside of her. The very man who had sworn to protect her was also the one that hurt her. Her dad insisted on disciplining her to the extreme, yet he had no discipline himself. She felt scared of him, rather than protected. She resented him, yet was more similar to him than to anyone else. She was stubborn; set in her ways.*

Whatever it had been lost out to the power of the ripples in the sand from last night's winds, as my attention diverted. I had heard those winds howling like a pack of wolves, all through the night. My mind bounced around like a ping-pong ball as my thoughts shifted, yet again. I wished I could just find a switch to turn that love off and put it to rest. Then maybe I could get some rest too.

I had become so transparent to Wayne. He had come to know me as a brother and he knew I was hurting inside. I glanced down into the coarse sand. Neither of us spoke a word. He gazed off into the distance, adjusting his vision through the small rectangles that made up the fence. He too, was caught in a daydream that transported him far from our stark reality – prison. The chatter of inmates could be heard in the distance; bustling about selling brownies, placing bets on football, and taunting one another over the card table. The smell of prison liquor, hooch as it was called, overwhelmed us each time Yardy popped the cap off the undercover soda bottle. My face scowled as I thought that such a drink couldn't possibly be healthy if the stench alone was so vulgar. It did its job though. The inmates were all laughing and telling jokes; red cheeks, watery eyes and all. They were all enjoying themselves while duck and goose were frozen in heartbreak. I closed my eyes and slipped off into a trance.

I heard the washing of dominoes two hundred meters away, along with the loud and obnoxious voice of West. He always slammed every domino he played. I imagined him shirtless, as he could always be found for some reason. His gray, speckled beard explained the old soul that he bore. His spirit also appeared happy, as he always kept those around him deep in laughter, as if he were hosting a Def Comedy Jam. Returning from my trance, I managed to pull together a soft smile and turned to see what Wayne was up to. Maybe it was just time to break the silence altogether. The indiscriminate noise was getting too loud and I was scared of listening to my own thoughts any longer. I knew they might continue to tell me the truth but I wasn't ready; it just wasn't the time. I already knew I had messed up over the years. I mean, just look at where I was. I needed no one to explain that to me – not even me!

My eyes scanned the room and landed on Wayne as he leaned against the antiquated phone box. His eyes were closed as if he was in a dream, but I knew all too well that he was only dreaming to lose his reality. As was the case with everything else around here, you had to fight even just to escape from your own mind for a minute and some Chicano was exemplifying just that. He had the nerve to ask Wayne for the phone that provided him comfort in that moment. When I realized what he was doing, I gave him mine to keep the peace. Just then, Wayne forced his eyes open just enough to observe the slim-built Mexican standing squarely in front of him and exclaimed, "Man get out of my face!"

The unrelenting thoughts running through my head had long since chased my smile away. *Maybe I was a bigot to love? How did I get here? Take a good look at yourself and your forefathers. Your father is a drunk. He lives with his wife but is separated and sleeps in an entirely separate room. Your grandfather is sophisticated, yet he's still a drunk. He too, lives with his wife yet sleeps without her. Was this what my life had in store for me?* This thought jolted me out of my dream-state. Why couldn't I fantasize like everyone else in here? They walked up and down these halls and filled them with smiles and laughter, as if they were at home with no worries.

Why was I so serious all the time? Herb got it right when he told me I was a chronic over thinker. *Was I even a dreamer*, I wondered? It's possible I was not but my forefathers sure were. If nothing else, it was a dream that bought my father's one-way ticket to federal prison for twenty years. My mother though, she was different as she preferred reality. "Work hard. Burn the midnight oil," she would always tell me. Whether she was running her small shop selling sweets, harvesting crops or raising animals, my mother led by example. It was through her determination alone that she was able to send me to Munro College, Jamaica's most prestigious secondary school.

My mom never thought I'd turn out just like her – blunt, harsh and fiercely independent. I stopped accepting money from her at fifteen years old but instead I bullied other kids at school, just as they'd done to me. I sold Gummy Bears to my classmates and I performed services for payment. Instead of waiting in long lunch lines, I would offer to put my connections to good use to retrieve and deliver lunches faster. Kids would pay me a fee for services such as this and this was how I made my money. I invested my money and bought a goat and a few pigs. My entrepreneurial spirit even led me to perform delivery duties where I brought weed to Kingston on school days. I made these deliveries to a relative's boyfriend and never spoke a word of it. I touched my second gun ever that same year. *Hard worker. Burning the midnight oil.* The principle was good, but I had no dreams and no goals; only fantasies. The sentimentalist in me was taught early on that dreams were impractical and led to nothing but disappointment; just like that time my grandmother promised me Nike Air Max's for Christmas but then sent me something different. Who wants to experience the high of a grandiose fantasy, only to be disillusioned shortly after?

That would never be me!

The reality is that I still struggled today. Who am I? One thing's for certain – my identity continues to evolve on a daily basis and didn't stop or slow once it crossed the line of felon. This label won't define me. Who shall I be? Where will my path lead? What will I become- a hard worker or a dreamer? Perhaps I will even be both.

Today, I am transferring to a new state prison and in true "manly" fashion, neither Wayne nor I spoke a word of it. We shared a bond. We had an unspoken love for one another but we just couldn't bring ourselves to say it. Maybe it was due to an ingrained fear of the prison culture we were immersed in. It was possible we had become soft. Whatever it was that day, we looked each other in the eye, speaking silently, all the while gazing through time.

FLORENCE WEST

———❦———

Exhausted, I peered through the window of the van. My view was of poor back roads in the middle of the desert. My eyes hung low, my body impetus to leave this confined space. My knees ajar to create less friction between the metal cage prohibiting access to the front of the van. The inmate sitting next to me drooled and bopped his head with every shrug of the van or obtrusive pothole. He never peered up once and his laziness permeated as I fell back asleep. As the van slowed, I woke up to see a huge coaster bus waiting. We had come to a complete stop before the Correctional Officers decided to ask if we had eaten all morning. They escorted us into separate cells and talked and laughed. I spun around to admire my environment. "Trees! Hell no," just bigger cactuses that I hadn't seen before. The prison complex must have been a maximum facility as no one was out but the few inmates they allowed to walk around as grounds crew. Even they were scarce.

After, the officers finished telling their jokes, they called the transport unit that was going to take us to our new homes. My mind raced. I wondered what lay outside of these walls. What city were we in? I was tired of being locked up. Tired of the same routine. Turn around, squat, and cough. Turn around, grab your nuts, pull them up, grab your ears, stick your tongue out, and run your fingers through your hair. The routine made me feel the dogs were more human than I; even they watched and smelled you for drugs.

Finally, the transport unit arrived. We were called by our names and number, patted down, then escorted onto a van or the big coaster bus. The bus was transporting inmates to Globe and Apache Complex. I made my way onto the van as it filled up.

Some inmates bragged, knowing where we were and gave their opinion based on our time left where we were headed. I was tired of the know-it-all mentality and kept quiet. I was exhausted; no one wanted my wrath if I was agitated by their meaningless conversation. It was the far-fetched introductions at county jail and entering prison all over. Who was in for what? It wasn't his first time. How many times they got away with the crime. Their friends are on this yard they're headed to. I forced a smile as I thought, "How dumb must I have been to be surrounded by people who didn't realize the one time they needed to get away, they didn't! We were in prison being treated less than animals because of our stupidity." If they didn't see the bigger picture, I sure did.

The van stopped at several prisons that were side-by-side. They finally arrived at Florence West. Home! The clouds masked the prison yard. It was abandoned. It resembled La Paz. Barren sand pit in the middle of the complex with a spectacular basketball court covered with a brawny aluminum roof. The Housing units looked smaller than what I was accustomed to, but my view was limited. We made our way into Arrival and were relieved of our jewelry: shackles and handcuffs. We were then stripped, searched, and were called one at a time to claim our property. To my misfortune, all my long-sleeved shirts were taken by the La Paz Officers. They noted that my shirts had not been ordered through property but was altered, which was illegal. Typical. What else did I lose?

At the end, I had everything else. The officers joked as they counted my food.

"Two bags. Wow! Somebody must really love you," the officer teased.

I was reserved as always. Not too quick to speak or make friends. I had gone through so much, I learnt to be patient with whom you occupy your time. We left all our property in arrival and were escorted to medical. We were all asked the same questions.

"Are you mentally ill? Do you take any meds? Are you thinking of hurting yourself?" The answer, "No! No! Hell, NO! I might have my days but I have life and a sound mind."

We returned to Arrival and were fed cold cut sandwiches. Sack lunches, as they are called, were the poor man's food. I hadn't eaten one in months, but no hot meal all day was enough to encourage me to gorge my own. I had no pride; I spun around for left overs that my good friends would donate. My eyes drooped as I thought of the journey from Yuma to Florence. I was so high-strung I hadn't slept all night. I longed for a bed. Cold concrete was becoming quite appealing, something I had vowed never to do. I hung on long enough. A female officer came and escorted us towards a fenced in side of the yard. The yard was opened as count was cleared.

I looked at the piece of paper that the officer in arrival handed me.

"Officer," I called to the female escorting us. "Why are we going to this little fenced in side of the yard?" I asked.

"This is two yards in one. This side is the DUI yard," she pointed to the larger side with the beautiful basketball court and large softball field. "This side is the Parole Violator's yard or for inmates with less than a hundred and twenty days," she ended, pointing towards Building Five that was all fenced in.

"Ricky. How much time you got left?" I asked. I knew him from La Paz.

"Three months, bro! Ending my six-year sentence," he ended. The officer stopped at the gate and got on her radio. In minutes, an officer came out of the building and opened the gate to let us in.

I was accustomed to DOC Officers wearing their khaki uniforms and macho bravado, but these officers were wearing blue shirts with 'Security' written in the back. The officer led us into the building. It was broken into four different pods, "A.B.C.D". My bed number was A44. I was pissed when I realized that all the bed areas were bunk beds. There were no cubicles. The whole pod was packed as a sardine can. Sixty men inside an area that resembles a basketball court spelt trouble. I found my bed and had a top bunk. Tired and mad was a recipe for disaster. My cellmate came running to help me. A youngster, tattoos all over his arms and face. He introduced himself and called himself Locc. I looked up and thought about bullying him immediately. He lacked confidence and it would be an easy victory. Something made me not do it. I questioned myself if this is how I wanted to start my day. "I thought you said you're a changed man." The thoughts lingered as I sat on his bed.

Me, 260 lbs. jumping up and down. Maybe the exercise was good. Even better, his foot wouldn't be stepping on my sheet as he went up and down.

"Bro! You're big as hell. If you want the bottom bunk, it's mine. I'm leaving Sunday, so you'll have it in four days anyways," he ended as I smiled.

I was happy to be alone. He was a West Side City Crip and I cared less about gang banging.

"Help me put those away, brother?" I sort of asked. "This is all I have as locker?"

I ended pulling the drawer so hard it clunked and echoed inside the pod. I looked up and realized all eyes were on my bags of food. Neville, a brother, came over and introduced himself. He helped me spread my mattress and we flung it on the top bunk.

"How long you've been here for, bro?" I asked.

"A couple of weeks. I'm back on a parole violation. I have three months to do and I'm glad I won't be on paper when I get out," he ended. He spun around and looked over his shoulder. "Watch out for Whistler because he has sticky fingers. We had to discipline him this weekend for stealing," he ended as we both laughed.

I wanted a bed tucked in at the back, but even though this bunk was upfront, it was bearable because I had no neighbor to my right.

It wasn't long before my cellmate and I put away all my food. My pairs of New Balances couldn't fit under my bunk or in my boxes. I didn't complain. New Balances meant you had money, two meant you're loved, three pairs and you're selling drugs or running a store. I hadn't received money from the streets since my incarceration. I rather any money that my loved ones or friends had for me go to my son. He needed it more than I. I was doing quite well based on prison standards. I walked outside to get a breather. Fresh air sent a wave of relaxation through my body. Before I knew it, everyone was being introduced. I met Patrice, Shaquille, and OG Fred that I knew from La Paz.

I spoke for a lengthy time as I got schooled on how this Yard operated. Everything trickled down from the bigger yard next door. They were the only ones that left the prison for jobs and they had the hook-up on everything. It wasn't long before my interest into how things operated was deemed suspicious. The conversation took a turn. They began asking about me. What was I in for? What yard was I on before? They were all fond about my bags of food and living with Whistler in A Pod.

"Don't kill him," they teased.

"I don't think that Whistler would be stupid enough to mess with him anyways," Patrice paused. "That man looks like he works out every day," he continued then ended.

"Mandatory," I exclaimed as they all laughed and talked about the weekend's events.

Even though the Yard was small, there were lots of fights and situations occurring. Patrice and Shaquille pulled me to the side. We walked to the basketball court on our side of the yard. It had one rim and no covers. It was made for eight-foot humans. The basket was so high you could catch an attempt to escape charge if you tried to dunk. Patrice was a six-foot-six, skinny Senegalese that was in for armed robberies. He was quite the pretty boy with his hair curly from chemicals. He had two aggravated armed robberies from robbing two banks. He bragged that the first teller liked him because she didn't testify and kept smiling with him. Shaquille was six-foot-two and was more laid back.

"Did you meet J Bones or Chief Locc?" Patrice asked.

"No!" I exclaimed.

I wondered why do I even need to know these people. I had never heard these names before.

"Chief Locc runs that side of the yard and J Bones runs this side," he said, looking around. "Even though it's split up what we do over here affects them on the other side." He stopped to catch the basketball that came our way. "We almost had a riot couple weeks ago because the Woods said a brother was cheating in poker. We were all ready to go and Chief Locc had all the brothers out." He paused. "It's been tense, since then," he ended.

I had interest in the underground market and what they were telling me I didn't care about. From what I understood, I needed someone on the other side of the yard. As I listened, I carefully watched how everyone maneuvered. Paying attention can save your life or tell you who's who!

"We'll introduce you to J Bones but I know Chief Locc would be glad to meet you," Patrice said with a grin.

"You know how he loves when we get some big brothers," Shaquille added as they laughed.

"Bro. What do you eat?" Patrice asked as he laughed. "Everything except pork," I answered.

"You big as hell," Shaquille said, grinning from cheek to cheek. "I've been eating everything, even beans and I can't get big, bro," Patrice said with a sigh.

"You Africans have a high metabolism, bro. That's why! Eat

more beans and rice," I ended.

"Listen, Bro. I know you didn't order that entire store you brought. You going to break out or what?" Patrice said, insinuating I was a part of the underground market. I pretended I didn't hear him. "Listen man, I got my money upfront." He went on rambling. I told him I didn't have anything a thousand times. "Jamaica! Reid! What's up, brother?" Tyson shouted.

I turned and saw this monster of a man. I knew him from La Paz also. He had done over ten years in DOC. He was the typical OG; huge triceps and chest but skinny legs from skipping leg day. We shook hands and he joined the conversation. He confirmed all the suspicions that Patrice and Shaquille had as he went on about my days at La Paz and how he'd purchased the best Spice from me.

"This dude almost got us into a riot. He's a good guy though. Always looking out for everyone. Don't I owe you?" he laughed. "Yeah, you do. A can of chew, honey buns, soda."

We all had a good laugh. I guess he'd thought I'd forget but I had an elephant's memory.

Time had flown by quickly as we began to catch up. After Tyson left, Patrice gave me the full introduction across the fence. In hours, I had all the information I needed to set the plan in action. Finally, I escaped their company and sat outside the building on the wall. I peered to my right. In my view were a McDonald's, a Sonic, and a Taco Bell under construction. The fragrance from Sonic was torture. Freedom was so close. The cars drove right next to the prison. The city noise could be heard as I thought of the next move. If I could have it my way, I'd like everything done without anyone knowing. That was the best way. I had learnt from dealing with Chuckie. Or so I thought.

Florence West Prison was right in the middle of Florence. There were over ten prisons inside the city. Private Prisons run by CCA, FCC, GEO, county jail, Juvenile Detention, State-run Prison, The Death Houses and a sex offender Yard. I was glad my cellmate wasn't going to be here longer because I was tired of his knucklehead mentality. I had no patience. I fed positive information and encouraged reading but listening to him speak was ridiculous.

"I'm banging the hood. The 'Big Homie' going to look out when I'm free," he repeated the same story all day.

He failed to realize that the true people that love us don't leave us alone in hell. If they hadn't been looking out, I doubt they would when he was free. I wanted to put him to my Spice game but I resorted to throwing him some soups. Fewer problems that way. I had met J Bones and traded all my cans of chew for food noting that he got a cut. He didn't leave an impression. He was jovial, loved playing table tennis, and got most of his food in hustling.

I decided to take a shower and realized there was no privacy. The officers looked directly into the pod. Their office was raised and situated in the middle of the building, giving a full view into all four pods. The only place that had some privacy was sitting on the toilet. Even then, your upper body could be seen. I took a shower and made something to eat. Ramen Noodles mixed with rice, tuna, and spicy squeeze cheese. A little hot sauce and it was perfect. I gave my cellmate some and went outside after count. I was starting to see that Florence had its setbacks but came with many perks. The yard was full of amenities.

The road was so close that everything was accessible. A burger from McDonalds wasn't farfetched if you paid the right price. A dollar burger might run you ten dollars. Ten soups, four tunas and the risk of being put on report if caught. There were cell phones and Spice everywhere. I lost somewhat of an interest when I heard how low the prices were. It was too high a risk for the return on investment. I went inside after a few minutes and had an early night.

Tap! Tap! Tap! I felt my bed vibrate. I woke up to everyone getting ready. I jumped up and asked my cellmate what was going on.

He ducked down from my facial expression.

"What's up, Bro? What's everyone doing up?" I asked rubbing my eyes. The window behind my bed had no sign of anything close to a sunrise. It resembled midnight.

"Breakfast, Bro. We eat at specific times. If you don't go now, you'll miss it," he informed and continued to get dressed.

I jumped down and threw on my shoes. I rubbed my eyes a few times. Everyone had already left as the officer yelled over the monitor, "Last Call!" I ran out the building and stopped under the Ramada to tie my shoes. Patrice and Shaquille were also behind.

"Yow, Bro! We were just looking for you," Patrice said, pulling up his pants as he walked in my direction.

"I thought it was going down this morning, bro. My cellmate was tapping mad hard on my bed. Why the hell ya'll get up so early for breakfast?"

Shaq and Patrice both laughed at me.

"We were both laughing last night as we knew you'd be mad as hell about these early breakfast. That's how this yard is brother," Shaquille explained. He seemed pretty level headed.

While we walked, we chatted and laughed. I saw some new faces and a few officers kept coming over to our table and asking information about the new inmate, me. My face told them all, "Get away from me." I was the most antisocial person in the mornings. Especially in prison.

The officers' biggest inquiry was how was I so big when there weren't any weights. They wanted to know how much I ran, what I ate, and how long my workout routine were, and how many times did I workout. We left the dining room together and I noticed that the DUI side of the yard was still closed. They were up peeking through their windows but couldn't venture outside. "Why they block us from talking with these inmates?" I asked out loud."

"They don't want us to mix. I guess that's why they fenced off Building Five. They said that inmates were coming from Building Five to the DUI yard beating up inmates and taking their store and property."

Shaquille spoke so calmly. He was unbothered or something else was on his mind. He was from New Jersey and came to Arizona for the same reason I did. He got in trouble with the law and was placed on probation. That led to him being unable to leave the state. Now he was serving a year for possession of firearm. He was prohibited from carrying a weapon because of probationary rules. He often joked that being in prison was unreal. He never thought in his life he would be a gun-toting gangster. He had big dreams in high school. He was good at basketball and saw himself going to college. Somehow, coming to Arizona for a vocation became a life sentence.

Getting back to Building Five, you were watched by multiple guards. Their eyes paced your every step and if you lagged behind, they would yell over the monitor to hurry up. We stopped under the Ramada after entering the gates to our building. As the last person entered, the gates were closed.

"I'm working out at 7am if anyone wants to join. First, let me tell you that I don't play while working out. If you're in, you're in for the long haul. There is no such thing as I can't. Let them muscles scream until they get tired," I ended my mini lecture.

They all laughed.

"Your workout is way too serious. What the hell! This isn't boot camp. You're talking like a drill sergeant," Shaquille laughed.

We talked for a while. I went inside and got dressed. Old tee shirt and shorts with fresh socks. I had so many socks. I bought a pair for a soup back at La Paz. New arrivals were the best bargain. A pair of socks cost $4.50 from the store but I got a pair for 60 cents from new arrivals.

I walked outside with my headphones over my ears. Music

blaring, I blocked everyone out. I was in the gym and was to be unbothered. I started by running two quick laps to warm up. Stretched my arms a bit then started doing pull ups. Ten sets then pushups and back arms. Working out using your body weight took some ingenuity. I was finishing my work-out by doing some extra sets of pull-ups. Maybe I impressed everyone by my stature, but my workout would speak for itself. I was stretching my arms out from being so tight when I saw a familiar face.

"New York!" I shouted and flung my hand in the air.

He was on the DUI side of the yard. He was walking laps with his friends and rapping. He yelled back.

"Rude Boyyyyy! What's going on, Brother?"

He walked to the fence and we did a two-finger handshake. We hadn't been talking for more than two seconds before the female in the visitation building yelled:

"Get back. One foot from the Fence!"

"Yeah, bro. They are petty here. They give tickets for nothing. Be careful," he suggested as we both backed away from the fence. "Thank you!" the female officer teased.

We spoke for a few minutes and decided to catch up later. He walked off yelling to his friends that I was a real Jamaican that he had met at County Jail. Little did he know my last words to him would not be what I myself would have thought.

I went straight inside and took a shower. Before I knew it, the yard was closed. I took a nap and was woken up by Patrice and Shaquille. They had no plans of going to lunch. They were serving cold cuts and nobody ate that. We made some chicken and tuna spread then ate together. Eating together, we talked about the parts of our lives that most around us didn't care to share. Shaquille was always absent mentally because his girlfriend was pregnant with his only child. She had written many letters explaining how stressful it is without him

Fighting Just to Dream

physically there as a support. Pretty boy Patrice had a wife but he was to be deported. He told her to move on with her life. Listening to them reflected my life. I had a son I was absent from physically and a girlfriend I hadn't spoken to or heard from in days. Maybe by now she was my ex. I found out Patrice and Shaquille didn't even smoke. They were the break down kings. They had the game on smash. That's how they survived. That's how most people survived, especially when they had no support from the street.

We came out of the building and met Chief Locc by the fence. "Stay back from the fence, Rude Boy! These people don't play about that," he ended after banging his whole set from Gardena Block California.

He was forty-two and had a record longer than my age. He was a Crip and a Muslim. He was the Head for the DUI side of the yard. He was a giant of a man with his face fully covered in tattoos. He wore his hair slicked back and in a ponytail. He was full of information about Black culture and history. I was immediately interested and forged a plan to study with him on the DUI yard. My excuse would be to say I'm going to medical then head to Building Four where he lived. He was very impressed by my knowledge and was surprised to hear me speak about topics he was interested in. We shared a passion for knowledge about the Black Man's Etymology.

Shawn, aka New York, came out and joined us. We repeated the stories of how we met in county jail. We were both in similar situations. We were both fathers who faced serving two and a half years in The Department of Corrections. I remembered Shawn writing his son's mother after he was sentenced. I could sense that reality had set in for him. I had helped him the night before sentencing to write a letter to his judge. The judge didn't even listen nor did his lawyer speak on his behalf to get a mitigated sentence. The judge still sentenced me to prison, but that was okay. I had finally taken responsibility for my life. -

"Yeah! Why you know him?" I asked.

Laughing he said, "That's Shaquille's cousin."

We both laughed. What were the odds? I had talked so much about looking out for Shawn, but Shaquille never said anything. Did he know all along and was just waiting to hear what I was going to say? Either way, I wasn't going to question him.

We walked to the dining hall when Shaquille joined us. I was a bit reserved. My thoughts were occupied by what may be going on outside the free world. Some days, it was hell inside my head. My thoughts had a mind of their own. I woke up feeling so energized but now a thought had taken me to away. Even my shoulders felt heavy. Mentally, I felt I had lost ten pounds of muscle mass. I felt fragile and thought everyone could feel my whole energy was off. I glided back to Building Five on autopilot. I never heard a word of the conversation. I just existed physically. I had to do something about this feeling. Patrice and Shaquille were ready to work out. I got changed and slapped my cheeks a couple times. I even tried talking to myself in the mirror. My last resort was to get my CD player and listen to some music. I came outside and waited on my work-out partners while coaching myself mentally. We ran a few laps to warm up then went straight into the routine.

All the anger and resentment that had paralyzed my mind made me physically numb. I was doing sets of workout routine as if I was half human half beast. Half way through the workout, Shaquille and Patrice slowed down. They really wanted to quit but I wouldn't let them.

"Don't try to do as much as I am. Do what you can but never give up! Keep going," I yelled and they did.

We ended and sat under the Ramada. The workout drove the crazy out and I regained my positive state of mind. My whole body paid the expensive price for my peace of mind. This was a regular routine. Mental torture was my best friend most days. You had to find some way to channel it to do well or you would not walk outside these gates with a sound mind. Before prison, I never took the time to even stop and think about things. What were my goals? What was success to me? What did I want from a relationship? What was love to me? Who was I?

The days faded and matched the days before. The same routine was what got to you if nothing else did. Time started to drag and Patrice was going home soon. Well, not quite! He was going to the Feds. Shaquille would be next, but for the time being, we made use of having each other. We started to sneak across to the DUI yard on Saturdays to play basketball. I met up with Chief Locc after the game and we decided on having *khutbahs* on Friday as well as embark on the journey of studying the *Etymology of the Black Man vs. TheBlack Man's Psychology*. Fridays and Saturdays had made my weekends flew by. I loved meeting with Chief. He was studying Psychology and he always had a way of asking me questions that made me stop and think before answering. I loved that he challenged me to grow. I worked hard and started to bring my own questions to our study time. That was the good side of things.

Standing by the fence, I noticed we were getting some new arrivals. I saw two brothers coming with their bags and yelled for someone to go help them. By the time the yard closed and we went back in, I found I had a new cellmate. His name was Cameron. He was Black and Mexican. 'Half-breed', as he called himself. He was California born but moved to Arizona to escape the gang violence. He was back on a violation. He had done three and a half years already for misconduct of weapons and discharging a firearm. We shared the same disgust for California Eses. His parole officer violated him for dirty urine. He was permitted to smoke because he had a medical marijuana card but they violated him anyway.He was pissed that he was away from his two sons again. He knew Neville from doing time on a different yard so we all became close friends. He wasn't a knucklehead and knew how to do time. We spoke a lot but never had any issues. If I was going to have a cellmate, I would have picked him myself.

Before long, Patrice had put me in touch with his runner, Casino. He owed me some money, and Patrice was counting down the time to when he thought I would beat him up. I didn't want to though. What I was learning with Chief Locc was of our forefathers selling us into slavery and killing each other because of tribalism. I wanted no part of the continued violence against my own kind or other races, but at times, I felt I wasn't given much choice.

Patrice was leaving soon and he warned me continually to get whatever I could from Casino. I wouldn't take half; I wanted it all because that way I wouldn't have to beat the shit out of him. "I bet he deuces up. That man looks terrified of you," he kept saying every time we spoke about it. I thought highly of Casino. He was claiming to be a GD from Chicago. The GDs that I had met were solid people so I afforded him some time to get his money together.

Patrice was leaving today. We ate breakfast and had some laughs. He wasn't worried about going to the Feds. He had already signed his deportation papers back to Senegal. Both Shaquille and I walked him to Property when they called him to leave. I saw the Federal Officers waiting outside the gates with their bracelets and chains. The white mini-van had no outward markings that I could see. I prayed that I wouldn't be leaving in that van.

Somehow, I believed there would be a miracle, but I also started writing a lot of people in power, including the President of the United States, Mr. Obama.

By the time we got back to the pod, Casino was taken and placed in protective custody. Shaquille started to laugh. I was furious. I hated when people did that. That's the golden rule; you don't break. I rather that man had come and spoken with me and let me know he couldn't pay me. I would have just written it off as bad debt and have him help me when I needed help doing laundry, cleaning my shoes, or helping out the older inmates on the yard. I sent word to him that he really let me down. Later, I found out that he was smoking meth and that was why he couldn't pay me. That explained what he had done.

Jay Love and Jay Bones left soon after and the atmosphere changed drastically. The Yard was more relaxed. Jay Bones was loud, and gambling all the time. OG Tyson had become Head, and he spoke very little and stayed to himself all the time. We would workout inside but other than that he slept, worked, and read books all day. He was a true veteran. He started persuading me to be the Head and I kept telling him no. He said either I would take it or anybody else he gave would have caused a riot. I told him I would think about it. I had in mind to ask Chief Locc what he thought. He was Head for quite a while. If anyone could give me some great advice it would be him.

Shaquille and I started hanging out more frequently after Patrice left. We started going to the fence together to meet up with Shawn. Shaquille was always mentally occupied with thoughts of his girlfriend who was pregnant. He needed to hear our conversations. He rarely spoke about his feeling towards her thinking he was the only one. He was so wrong. He was fooled by the facades that everyone wore. Their shell of a life was so fragile all you had to do was broach on a sensitive topic. For most, that was talking about their family or partner. For the most part, Shawn had grown a lot from the conversations we used to have in county. I loved that. He had more than enough time to think. He had spent two weeks in the hole for possession of prison contraband.

"The walls were talking to me, bro. When that stopped, I started talking to myself. I was scared for a minute so I shut up. Then the silence became so loud," he ended.

I understood him totally. I had a similar experience in Walley

Correctional Complex when I was being housed for extradition in New Haven, Connecticut. I remember yelling to the guard and banging on the door like a mad man. Spit flying out my mouth, eyes bulging, and the bottom of my fist was sore from the continuous impact on the lavish metal door. I did two days in that cell and that was enough to register as being legally crazy.

However, I believed it all helped me. That was the first dose of getting to know myself. The longer spell of being introduced into the Department of Corrections was an eye opener. I started seeing life in a whole different way. I was confident in myself needing no camaraderie to state my opinion or just to say no to a lot of the negatives that surrounded me. Many had tried to get me to smoke and drink. When that didn't work, they wanted me to walk around beating everyone by spreading gossip and small talk. I had control of myself, no one else, and as long as I remembered that I didn't need to prove a thing to anyone. It occurred to me that the people that hurt others were hurting themselves. I guess that's why they say 'misery love's company'.

I began sharing a blog post I had written on the yard. The topic I came up with was, "I am an African American." Lindsey had helped me set up my website and I had begun to write blog posts weekly. I read it aloud to Shaquille and Shawn and they both loved it. It was explaining the mentality of the Black Man. Our focus on the White man: who's weaker? Who's stronger? Slavery. Gentrification. White power! Black power. Fighting over hue. We were so focused on the negatives that we failed to realize all we have control over is ourselves, yet we keep playing victim and focusing on the negative propaganda that sells so well. I wanted none of it anymore. I wanted personal growth through continued self-development. After reading my blog post, positive thoughts began to flood my brain. I wanted more of this positivity. It gave me a high I couldn't get enough of.

Christmas had arrived and I hadn't received a word from my girlfriend. I prayed for her as usual. Wishing her and her family the best Christmas ever. A part of me wanted to call but the mental abuse I had been through didn't warrant her that luxury. A different time maybe. At least she had family and friends that would be around her. I had no one. My closest family was three thousand miles away. Nevertheless, Shaquille and I made do with what we had. The exotic dish of clams and oyster with lemon tilapia was our Christmas meal. We ate and bought cold sodas after and celebrated Christmas prison style. In two days, Shaquille would be a free man. I was happy for him but a little jealous. I missed my family; I missed brushing my teeth with a mechanical toothbrush. I missed freedom.

I started a stringent routine. I made no time for anything negative. I had someone sell all the drugs for me. I called Lindsey for more books. I was yearning for information. While on my bunk reading, I decided to take a break. I filled a bottle of water up and sat on my bed. I turned around to admire the view outside. The sun centered the sky and its rays penetrated the dry, sandy soil. There were a few people working out outside. I couldn't even bear the sun much less workout in it. Whether it was winter or summer, Arizona wasn't my favorite place. I recognized we had gotten a new brother. He was tall with long dreads and wore glasses. He worked out like a seasoned prisoner going through his routines. Using the limited stations we were given, one had to be clever to work out specific muscle groups.

I finished my reading and decided after count was cleared that I would introduce myself to the new brother. He introduced himself as Amani Sosa but preferred to be called Jack Rabbit. He spoke very educated and had a wealth of knowledge as we broached on many topics. He had read quite extensively over the past years. Over a thousand books had been added to his credit. He had done over ten years in the Department of Correction. His felonies listed from felony flight to armed robbery. He had done three separate terms and vowed this was his last. He had lost his wife, his four sons, his girlfriend, and promised never to lose himself. He was very skeptical. He had seen me around for a couple days but avoided me because of the fear inmates had of me.

"When I see you talking to people, brother. You don't see the look people have on their faces. When I see how they all react to you, I told myself I'm staying away from you. I don't fear you or anything of that sort. I just thought you were an angry bird bullying everybody like your name D-Bo."

We both laughed heavily. As time had passed, he realized I just didn't have time for the nonsense.

We started discussing the books both he and I had read. He was interested in writing but had lost the copy of a book he had written and wanted to use his time to re-write his book. I was elated we shared a passion for writing. His book was titled *A Man Like Me*. It was giving the male perception of a healthy relationship. Its chapters were of the most important elements to a relationship. He was quite aware of the many books depicting what women needed. He wanted women to be able to understand that men desire certain elements in a relationship also. He had many valid points and I helped him brainstorm a bit to increase his ideas. Before I left, he asked for some Spice to smoke. I couldn't fathom the idea that such a man would indulge in something so unhealthy. I was purely aghast.

Inside my pod, I was pacing through my thoughts. What to do? For the first time, I felt guilty for selling Spice. Before, there was always a reason for my involvement. They were addicts anyway. If I didn't supply it, then somebody else would. Better Spice than heroin or meth. For the very first time, I severely questioned my involvement. Jack wasn't an addict; he didn't look or act like one. He knew all the repercussions and still wanted to smoke it. Just for a temporary relief, he risked everything.

I sent someone to give it to him. The whole time I laid in my bed unable to read. My book lay on my chest as I gazed at the water-spotted ceiling. For a second, I returned to judge my actions in favor of what I did. It didn't last, I came back to the conclusion this was wrong. How dare I encourage people to read, to learn, to do and grow but yet supply them with poison to break down the very thing I encouraged them to build? I was such a hypocrite. Preaching positivity, encouraging it but on the other hand supplying one of their biggest downfalls: drugs.

I tried to work it all out in my head. He wanted it. Nobody even forced him to smoke Spice. He wasn't scared to ask me, even though many thought I was intimidating. He probably needed it. He needed to medicate because he had done over ten years. Most inmates after completing five years are diagnosed with PTSD. Shit, you only need to do six months to qualify for PTSD. It was his sedative. After all, which one of us was perfect? I sure wasn't, so who was I to judge anyone else? Somehow, I still couldn't shake the feeling so I decided to talk to Jack.

"Why do you smoke that stuff, bro? You know all that it does and you still do. That shit kills brain cells, causes strokes and epileptic attacks!" I ended with an exclamation point.

Maybe he would finally get it if I said it to him.

"Brother, I know this stuff is bad but I rather float through the day rather than sit all day and worry what is going on outside." Jack looked down in a worry. "I just got this apartment and they violated my parole. Now I don't know if I'll have the apartment when I get out. I don't want to leave prison and be homeless." He sighed heavily. "I don't know what these people want me to do. I hope they let me out when I get to see the parole board," he ended.

For the first time, I had nothing to say. I had never experienced such a thing. The system continuously seemed all wrong. We were here and they made money from us. You're released and you have to pay for UA, pay rent at the half way house and work and check in constantly. If you were released on probation, you had to pay probation fees. Where was the support as a returning resident to become a successful member of society? We decided to work out together to let off some steam. The only solution I could find was to support my brother by getting him physically strong and encourage him to stop smoking. He did eventually. He had wanted to all along. A few brothers left and they were replaced by others. Brownie, a Chicano I knew from La Paz, arrived to the yard. He was a drug addict. He violated parole for a dirty UA and absconded. He sold drugs for anyone to stay in the thick of things so he could get his fix, whatever the drug was. We knew each other but I didn't do business with him. Some people were bad for business and he definitely was.

Working out with Jack allowed me to learn a lot about the struggles he had faced. He had watched his father die from cancer in a matter of months. His father was his everything and at a young age Jack rebelled against society's conforms. He was very humble but never scared. He bragged about his large forearm and what a damage it could and had done. He gave me a list of books to read. *Think and Grow Rich* was the headliner. In a day, I had read the book and found it quite interesting. There were some psychological effects to it that I loved. The next was Steven Covey, *The Seven Habits of Highly Effective People*. I started to see a familiar pattern between the content I was reading and my personal writings. My quotes also reflected a lot of the material I covered. I continued with the *Richest Man in Babylon* and *Creativity- Unleashing the Powers Within '*. I instinctively brought *Creativity* to Shawn, seeing that he was an aspiring rapper that he would benefit from such material. Reading *Brainwashed* was a game changer as it grew my outlook on racial issues.

Jack and I embarked on a personal discovery. We read a book or two a day. No matter the content we read, we collaborated our brains to create new ideas. I had come to a point in my life where even though I was informed and felt as I've grown, I was still stuck. I went to bed with this puzzling thought. I woke up at 4:30am crying my eyes out. I felt so joyful but I was crying like I've never cried before. I didn't even care if Cameron or anyone around me heard. I cried until the sun started to rise. I got on my knees and started praying. After I grabbed my diary and started writing.

'THE SPIRIT IN ME.'

The spirit in me cries to be truly free. It's as if the light of the world shines through me. I feel peace, calm, loved, and loving all. A true friend I have indeed' -01.09.2016.

I immediately opened my locker and grabbed a notepad. I started to write a letter to my ex-girlfriend. I began explaining that I'm writing this letter as a friend. I wanted her to know that I was sorry for all the things I'd done. This process allowed me to complete the journey of forgiveness. I had to forgive her and myself. I had to forgive us both because the anger and resentment was holding me back from growing. I was caught up in all the facades of the word. Trying to be strong, I found strength in letting go.

It was for the first time I felt truly free. I was walking the yard smiling from cheek to cheek. I was encouraging people selflessly to be aware of the negative propaganda they held secure to. To let go of them all felt amazing. To let ourselves be free and to be the best version we could be. We had been taught to be tough and strong because we were men. I begged to differ and discredited everything that my own perceptions had created limitations. I was fueled and marched on preaching my new way of life. I began a journey to study who I was. Man? What was our definition? What was our purpose? What was my whole existence about? I labored on combining all my resources.

I worked day and night like a mad man. I watched no television and gave it to my good friend Fred. He was serving time for drug possession. He both sold and used drugs. His drug of choice was crack and I begged him continuously to stop. He continued to use and all I could do was inform him of the effects and be a positive friend. Jack and I, meanwhile, began writing our books. He had a new-found respect for my outlook. He felt

I had literally changed overnight. He thought I didn't even sound aggressive as I used to. I wasn't all the way there but I had slowed down a bit. I had asked him to follow in my footsteps. I asked him to write a letter to everyone that had hurt him and one to himself. I told him about the relief he would feel and that his book wouldn't be from just a broken perspective. He accepted my challenge and felt so much better after writing his letters.

Jack abruptly stopped working out with me one morning. He decided he wanted to work out at a different time. He suggested I was very complicated. He had known me for months now and didn't understand me. Great, I didn't even understand me. He thought I had three conversations all the time. One with the person I was talking to. The other conversation was with myself. Thirdly, were the facts that I deemed truthful and believed to be real.

"Brother! Now I know why your girl left you. Man, you're so difficult to understand, then with your loquacious personality one can easily get frustrated because they misunderstand you. I thought I knew you, but man, you're selfish too. You want to work out when you want to. You want to work on the things you like. You're so open but yet so closed off. I don't understand." He paused and shook his head. "Brother, sometimes you wake up and you won't speak for hours but you keep smiling. People around here keep asking me, 'What is Reid smiling so much about'? I tell them that the man is blessed and highly favored but they still don't understand. They don't see things the way you do. Brother, you are not supposed to be in this environment at all. Your education is beyond what most of these inmates would understand. Most of these people are seasoned criminals. They don't want to hear what you're saying most of the time. They look at you as being cocky, thinking you are better than them." He stopped to point at Fred. "All he wants is a TV, his Spice, and he will sleep his time away. You think he cares about being proactive or productive. That man looking at you like, 'Boy, I can't wait to leave here to be proactive selling more drugs'. They don't see the bigger. Get them to see the bigger picture and then you'll have something going," he ended.

He sat down on his bed and I pondered on the information I had received. You know what too, bro. Go tell those people you don't want to be Head anymore". In Florence, the officers knew who the Heads were and it was ok. He wanted me to denounce my role in the prison politics. He thought it was a trap.

Jack had made great points. I understood he was trying protect me, but he hadn't realized I wasn't scared anymore. I wasn't scared to be myself. I could tell the truth and be comfortable. I could represent my race as Head because I was doing it purely and without gain. I wanted to better everyone. I was tired of the broken script. Racial segregation.

Seasoned convicts, Gang bangers, hustlers and gangsters. I wanted everyone to be able to leave here with a plan to succeed. I wanted them to develop an idea and work it into a masterpiece. I wanted them to see that this was just a time to get to know themselves and there was much more to life that what our temporary world presented. Being a Head wasn't entirely my plan but I was encouraged to take the role by Chief Locc and Tyson. I viewed it in a positive sense. I was the CEO of a large corporation managing and improving the company's productivity. I was helping others stay out of trouble and in turn helping myself because that was one less race riot I had to worry about.

My days flew by even after I was given extra time as my earliest release date was taken away. I remained focused and productive. I was writing more now than ever. My writing had grown. I was opening up a lot more intrinsically. It reflected me; my conscious and unconscious thoughts but I laid a pattern. I was truly joyful to be alive and for the first time, I truly felt I loved myself. I decided to write about the love that I felt that wasn't limited or held conditions. I shared my writings and called Shawn to the fence. He had gotten a little heavier. He had started working out with Chief Locc. My post blew him away.

"Brother Jamaica. That's fire. You know what. The other day Kayray was talking about you. He has never met someone so consistent as you are. Always preaching positivity, self-awareness and just informing everyone around you. He said you turned down a lot too." He paused. "That'sgood though, brother. I know you were carrying some demons like we talked about. Feeling abandoned in here can take its toll on anyone."

He had been fighting his own battles himself. He still hadn't heard a word from his son's mother. He had been getting into fights and I knew that was the cause. I listened to him speak for a while just so he could vent his frustrations. He was feeling better by the time the Yard was closed. We did our two-finger handshake and headed inside. I thought of the book *Houses of Healing* and ran back to the fence to give an inmate to give to Shawn. I hoped he would take the time to read it. I didn't have much luck with getting inmates to read. Some just didn't have the time while serving time and had nothing to do but sit and chill all day. If one was going to be a successful member of society, I believe it was imperative to understand time management and blocking out the excessive noise that surrounded us.

I began attending church with Jack. I met one of the most incredible men at our first meeting. Pastor Rob was a Grizzly bear of a man but had such a gentle voice. He didn't preach as the righteous disciple but entirely as a sinner. An imperfect man, working to become perfect. I could understand his message and we became very close. I had shared with him that I had no religion for the purpose that it brought division. He concurred and I was so surprised to know that he felt the same. Jack was getting close to his release and Pastor Rob was his second avenue of positive reassurance. Jack finally got some good news that the girl he was talking to had kept up with his rent payments and that he would still have his apartment when released. I was happy he had one less thing to worry about.

Pastor Rob became both our mentors. He encouraged us to share our stories so other inmates would understand but at first I was reluctant not knowing the bible as others did. Jack and Chief Locc started encouraging me to preach and I became very taken aback that both men thought the same of me. Chief Locc loved how I carried myself and said I had a voice that made everyone stop and listen. Jack just thought I had this animalistic attraction about me that drew people to me. He referred his assumptions back to a day when the Prison Therapist came and sat with me under the Ramada and told me her life story. Jack had gotten up and left after she began because he thought she was trying to have a private conversation with me. We both thought about it for a while until I decided to not act quickly but rather continue to develop the right habits and moral principles, which would lead to a better character.

As Jack got closer, he began to be relaxed. He slept most of the day and I continued to labor on. He was resting. He knew he would have to get to work when he was released. I had a different concept. I was working now so that when I'm released, I'm ahead of the ones just starting out. My philosophy was there is no such thing as luck. Luck was grinding it out until the opportunity and preparedness collided. I believed I was the miracle I'd always been looking for. Once I adapted this mindset, I started seeing opportunities everywhere.

Everything had a separate meaning to it and could be developed. I began taking a piece of paper and a pen with me everywhere I went. I was like a madman. I was definitely not the norm and it proved I wasn't as I began exclusively hitting out about racial segregation.

Before I knew it, I was in a meeting with all the other Heads talking to the Deputy Warden about changes in the ADC. They all stated that it would never change and that this is how it always was and would be. I found it strange that men thought like this in 2016. I stated my personal opinion that segregation is breeding hatred among inmates and brings about a superiority and inferiority complex. Once that was established, it was no wonder so many inmates would die from racial riots. All the other Heads looked at me as if I was crazy so I quickly stated that this is my opinion and that it didn't reflect the opinion of my race.

By the time we got back to the pod, we were all summoned to have our own meeting. Relly was my right hand in these situations so he accompanied me to the recreation room. The door closed and the meeting was convened. They all stated that their Heads from higher yards had sent down the word to not comply. The only reason they didn't want this to end was because they got money from taxing the smaller yards. The whole system was that of politicians on Capitol Hill. I refused to join and said I held firm to my opinion. Brownie seemed to have an issue and I wished he would say something but unfortunately, he didn't.

The meeting was adjourned and Relly loved it. He was glad I didn't agree with them. He had been on higher yards and wouldn't even speak with them but that was because the Woods and Chicanos ran most yards because they had the larger population. If that were to break down, they couldn't hide behind anything anymore.

Jack continued to beg me to leave the whole situation alone. I just couldn't. I had to stand up for something, even if it meant I would be in harms' way.

"These people are cowards, bro. They are hiding behind this whole race issue. Tell them face you one on one and the whole story changes to, 'I don't have an issue, brother. I was just saying'. Bull shit!" I yelled. I screamed so the whole pod could hear me.

"Calm down, Bro," Jack intervened. "You're seeing it from your angle but think about it. None of us would ever let anybody come in here and do anything to you. I know we going to knock some heads off, but what about the casualty? You have to think about that. To be honest, brother, you have so much to share with the world I don't want you to let your passion get the best of you to be stopped here. These people would love nothing but that. That's a victory to them when you can get out and reach millions. Think about it?" he asked rhetorically. "Martin Luther King Jr. Malcolm X, died from their passion."

I thought about it and I really didn't mind dying, but he had a point. Death was the easy way out. I had to have discipline. I grabbed my prison diary and began to write:

> Today, I made the decision to live to influence others and myself positively. The problem isn't black and white but it's answer is simply 'wrong or right". The God I serve is Love, and Love has no hatred or resentment; therefore, I should love all men, no matter what they have done to me. Hatred eats at our soul. It divides us and tears us apart from Human dignity. I chose to live. I chose life.

Jack was gone and I stayed to myself and continued my routine. I remembered Jack's last words to me while we walked to Property.

"When I realized I was heading back to prison, I asked God to make sure he put me with someone that would help me grow. Brother, I've met a lot of men over ten years and you are above all that I've met. I've never been so truthful with anyone before. Not even my own girlfriend. It was good, though, because at my weakest and most vulnerable moments, I became strong. I have no doubt you're blessed and highly favored. I believe in you, brother. I know you will be a great man. You are a KING!" he exclaimed.

I was happy to know that my brother was free. Free to choose and decide his fate. I would be free soon but the thought didn't occupy my mind. I had work to do and work I did. The ideas kept flowing and before I knew it, my birthday had arrived. I received so many birthday cards and letters I felt so appreciated. I even received two cards from Jack. He was out and doing well. He got his old job back and was focused. I told him to never forget the days when we were told to go to bed, when to get up, and what we had to eat. Let that memory serve as his motivation and work his plan to perfection. Let no one distract him. As I wrote him, I decided to take my own advice.

I woke up for breakfast. This was my final day in Arizona Department of Corrections. I had given away all my property the night before. Most of my brothers complained that I gave everything to Shawn. They didn't understand the bond I shared with him. He was my little brother and I didn't try to let them understand either. The most important parts of meI had given them: The Truth. The Truth why I was here and what I had done. What I was setting out to do. The truth of what drives me. The true emotions that I had shared. My life story written on paper for everyone. My dreams written in poetic form. Most importantly, my perspective on prison. It wasn't the end. We can all make it. Each one teaches one and to walk the talk. Execute the promises we made to ourselves. Many thought prison was a struggle, but in all honesty, it was always a struggle whether free or not. Gather that mindset and promise yourself to put one foot in front of the other at all times and you'll find your path much more clear with a lot of life's blessings.

Holding my box graffitied all over it from my friends' signatures, I walked to Property. Jay brought my bedding. It was customary for the prisoner leaving to never bring his own bedding. I scampered up the track in a relaxed state. I wondered what lay ahead of me.

Shawn and Kayray joined me in my walk. Hustle Man stopped by to say his goodbyes. It felt good as every few steps another brother or even other races would bid me farewell. The Lieutenant came and yelled," Let's go!" I dapped Shawn and walked inside. He too would do this exact routine in a matter of months. The feeling wasn't as I expected. I had a still calmness about me. I signed my freedom and put on my sweat suit I had worn to Arizona for court. Next, I was walking towards the gate a free man. I never looked back, even when Shawn and Kayray yelled to me. I yelled back to them, exclaiming that the manliest thing I had done in prison was to cry.

Through the square rectangles in the fence, I saw a white minivan pull up. Two Federal officers came out and started to pull out chains and handcuffs. The gates opened, they asked my name and told me to turn around. I requested that I get shackled with hands on the van because there is no way I was looking back where I had just come from. He obliged and I was sitting in the back of the minivan. As they drove off, I wondered what was next in the tale of my story.

Errol R. Reid

LETTER TO YOU

Where do I begin? The many sins I've committed against you? The love that I still have for you or the memories of wrongs and abandonment I've felt by you. How could I dare do such a thing? You've done so much for me when I needed everything. A place to lay my head and a body to cuddle with. I honestly have to come to terms with myself; I was the problem. None of us is perfect, but I can only speak for myself. I have seen how much I've hurt you and in turn hurt me too.

My communication was so poor. I got angry when I wanted to tell you 'Hold me' and a big 'I love you'. One second, I was the best, the next I was the worst. You asked me for security but I wasn't even secure of myself. My identity was a fake, a camouflage to survive because that's what the life I lived required. A question you asked sparked a fire. It made me want to know myself. To truly see and be the best I can be. One question I wish I could ask is," Did you see what I've become in me?"

I've taken this journey alone but I truly wish you could see me. I am still a work in progress but that's what makes me perfect, perfectly incomplete. I now know who I am, my purpose, and with God involved, I'm bound for greatness and great victory. The struggles I felt, the pain, it was all real but it was necessary because it was needed to be the best I can be. I cried for you, I missed you, I felt at times I needed you, but I needed God and He alone provides all we need.

I see how control is somewhat of a myth because who can you control but yourself for everyone and everything else is going to do and be who they want to be. I've lost everything but found myself and that is truly priceless, very priceless to me. A man that knows himself needs not do anything to prove to none else. Thank you, I miss you. I pray you be all you can be.

ABOUT THE AUTHOR

Born in Mandeville, Manchester, Jamaica as the youngest of three siblings, I was ushered into a life of perpetual struggle. Nevertheless, grit coupled with ambition and education afforded me a seat at Munro College, one of Jamaica's most prestigious high schools. I proudly represented the school in soccer, earning accolades and international recognition, culminating with a spot on Jamaica's National U20 team. Upon graduating, I packed my single bag of belongings and began my life anew in America as I was recruited by Post University in Waterbury, CT. Little did I know at the time, that place was going to change my life for the worst before it yet again changed it for the best! Grappling with the massive financial burdens of an international student fighting to stay afloat in a foreign country, on his own, I began selling marijuana. My previous endeavors landed me on medal podiums while this one landed me in state prison. My story had only just begun.

Errol R. Reid